Songs of Fellowship

BOOK FIVE

WORDS EDITION

KINGSWAY MUSIC

EASTBOURNE

The words of most of the songs in this publication
are covered by the Church Copyright Licence

United Kingdom
CCL UK Ltd, P.O. Box 1339, Eastbourne, East Sussex, BN21 4YF

United States
CCL Inc., 6130 NE 78th Court, Suite C11, Portland, Oregon 97218

Australasia
CCL Asia Pacific Ltd, P.O. Box 1254, Castle Hill, NSW 2154

ISBN 0 85476 550 6
(Music edition ISBN 0 85476 549 2)

Produced by Bookprint Creative Services
P.O. Box 827, BN21 3YJ, England for
KINGSWAY MUSIC LTD
Lottbridge Drove, Eastbourne, E. Sussex BN23 6NT
Printed in Great Britain

1

ALL CONSUMING FIRE,
You're my heart's desire,
And I love You dearly, dearly Lord.
You're my meditation,
And my consolation
And I love You dearly, dearly Lord.

Glory to the Lamb,
I exalt the great I AM;
Reigning on Your glorious throne,
You are my eternal home.

2

ALL I ONCE HELD DEAR, built my life upon,
All this world reveres, and wars to own,
All I once thought gain I have counted loss;
Spent and worthless now, compared to this.

Knowing You, Jesus,
Knowing You, there is no greater thing.
You're my all, You're the best,
You're my joy, my righteousness,
And I love You, Lord.

Now my heart's desire is to know You more,
To be found in You and known as Yours.
To possess by faith what I could not earn,
All surpassing gift of righteousness.

Oh to know the power of Your risen life,
And to know You in Your sufferings.
To become like You in Your death, my Lord,
So with You to live and never die.

3

ALL THAT I AM *I lay before You;*
All I possess, Lord I confess
Is nothing without You.
Saviour and King, I now enthrone You;
Take my life, my living sacrifice to You.

Lord, be the strength within my weakness;
Be the supply in every need,
That I may prove Your promises to me,
Faithful and true in word and deed.

Into Your hands I place the future;
The past is nailed to Calvary,
That I may live in resurrection power,
No longer I but Christ in me.

4

ALL THE ENDS OF THE EARTH will
remember,
And turn to the Lord of glory;
All the families of the nations will bow
down to the Lord,
As His righteous acts of power are
displayed.

And we will awaken the nations,
To bring their worship to Jesus.
And righteousness and praise shall
spring forth
In all the earth.
And we will awaken the nations,
To bring their worship to Jesus,
And the kingdom shall be revealed in
power,
With signs, wonders and miracles,
And righteousness and praise shall
spring forth
In all the earth.

Who will not fear the Lord of glory,
Or bring honour to His holy name?
For God has spoken with integrity and truth,
A word which cannot be revoked.

5

AND HE SHALL REIGN *forever,*
His throne and crown shall ever endure.
And He shall reign forever,
And we shall reign with Him.

What a vision filled my eyes,
One like a Son of man.
Coming with the clouds of heaven
He approached an awesome throne.

He was given sovereign power,
Glory and authority.
Every nation, tribe and tongue
Worshipped Him on bended knee.

On the throne forever,
See the Lamb who once was slain.
Wounds of sacrificial love
Forever shall remain.

6

ANOINTING, FALL ON ME,
Anointing, fall on me;
Let the power of the Holy Ghost
Fall on me,
Anointing, fall on me.

Touch my hands, my mouth and my heart,
Fill my life, Lord, every part;
Let the power of the Holy Ghost
Fall on me,
Anointing, fall on me.

7

AS WE BEHOLD YOU, as we behold You,
We are changing into Your image.
As we behold You, as we behold You,
We are changing from glory to glory.

As we behold You in all of Your glory,
Lord, by Your Spirit we are changing
Into Your image from glory to glory,
As we behold You, living God.

8

AT THE FOOT OF THE CROSS,
I can hardly take it in,
That the King of all creation
Was dying for my sin.
And the pain and agony,
And the thorns that pierced Your head,
And the hardness of my sinful heart
That left You there for dead.

And O what mercy I have found
At the cross of Calvary;
I will never know Your loneliness,
All on account of me.
And I will bow my knee before Your throne,
'cause Your love has set me free;
And I will give my life to You, dear Lord,
And praise Your majesty,
And praise Your majesty.

9

BE FREE *in the love of God,*
Let His Spirit flow within you.
Be free in the love of God,
Let it fill your soul.
Be free in the love of God,
Celebrate His name with dancing.
Be free in the love of God,
He has made us whole.

For His purpose He has called us,
In His hand He will uphold us.
He will keep us and sustain us
In the Father's love.

God is gracious, He will lead us
Through His power at work within us.
Spirit, guide us, and unite us
In the Father's love

10

BEHOLD THE LORD upon His throne;
His face is shining like the sun.
With eyes blazing fire, and feet glowing
    bronze,
His voice like mighty water roars.
Holy, holy, Lord God Almighty;
Holy, holy, we stand in awe of You.

The first, the last, the living One,
Laid down His life for all the world.
Behold He now lives for evermore,
And holds the keys of death and hell.
Holy, holy, Lord God Almighty;
Holy, holy, we bow before Your throne.

So let our praises ever ring
To Jesus Christ, our glorious King.
All heaven and earth resound as we cry:
'Worthy is the Son of God!'
Holy, holy, Lord God Almighty;
Holy, holy, we fall down at Your feet.

11

BE KNOWN TO US IN BREAKING BREAD,
But do not then depart;
Saviour, abide with us, and spread
Thy table in our heart.

There sup with us in love divine;
Thy body and Thy blood,
That living bread, that heavenly wine,
Be our immortal food.

12

BLESSÈD BE THE NAME OF THE LORD,
Blessèd be the name of the Lord,
Blessèd be the name of the Lord most high!
Blessèd be the name of the Lord,
Blessèd be the name of the Lord,
Blessèd be the name of the Lord most high!

The name of the Lord is a strong tower,
The righteous run into it,
And they are saved.
The name of the Lord is a strong tower,
The righteous run into it,
And they are saved.

Glory to the name of the Lord…

Holy is the name of the Lord…

13

BLESSÈD JESUS come to me,
Soothe my soul with songs of peace.
As I look to You alone
Fill me with Your love.

Glorious, marvellous
Grace that rescued me;
Holy, worthy
Is the Lamb who died for me.

Mountains high and valleys low,
You will never let me go;
By Your fountain let me drink,
Fill my thirsty soul.

14

BLESS THE LORD, MY SOUL,
And bless His holy name.
Bless the Lord, my soul,
He rescues me from death.

It is He who forgives all your guilt,
Who heals every one of your ills,
Who redeems your life from the grave,
Who crowns you with love and compassion.

The Lord is compassion and love,
Slow to anger and rich in mercy.
He does not treat us according to our sins,
Nor repay us according to our faults.

As a father has compassion on his children,
The Lord has pity on those who fear Him;
For He knows of what we are made,
He remembers that we are dust.

15

BREATHE ON ME, Spirit of Jesus.
Breathe on me, Holy Spirit of God.

Fill me again, Spirit of Jesus.
Fill me again, Holy Spirit of God.

Change my heart, Spirit of Jesus.
Change my heart, Holy Spirit of God.

Bring peace to the world, Spirit of Jesus.
Bring peace to the world, Holy Spirit of God.

16

BUT IF WE WALK IN THE LIGHT
As He is in the light,
We have fellowship with one another,
And the blood of Jesus His Son
Purifies us from all sin.

17

CALLED TO A BATTLE, heavenly war;
Though we may struggle, victory is sure.
Death will not triumph, though we may die;
Jesus has promised our eternal life.

By the blood of the Lamb we shall
overcome,
See the accuser thrown down.
By the word of the Lord we shall
overcome,
Raise a victory cry,
Like thunder in the skies,
Thunder in the skies.

Standing together, moving as one;
We are God's army, called to overcome.
We are commissioned, Jesus says go;
In every nation, let His love be known.

18

CLAP YOUR HANDS, ALL YOU NATIONS,
Shout to God with cries of joy,
O how awesome is the Lord most high,
The King over all the earth!

He subdued nations under us,
The peoples under our feet,
And He chose our inheritance for us,
The pride of Jacob, whom He loved.

Now our God has ascended
In the midst of shouts of joy,
And the Lord is in among the trumpet
    sound,
Among the trumpet sound!

Sing praise to God.
Sing praises to the King,
Sing praises to the King.
(Repeat)

For our God is King of all the earth,
Sing Him a psalm of praise,
For He rules above the nations on His
    throne,
On His holy throne.

All the people are gathered
Of the God of Abraham,
For the kings of all the earth belong to God,
And He is lifted high!

19

CLOSER TO YOU, Lord, and closer still,
Till I am wholly in Your will.
Closer to hear Your beating heart,
And understand what You impart.
O Breath of life, come purify
This heart of mine and satisfy.
My deep desire is to worship You,
Lord of my life, come closer still.

20

COME, HOLY SPIRIT,
Come, Holy Spirit,
Come to this place,
We will embrace Your presence.

Come, soften our hearts,
Come, soften our hearts,
That we may obey,
Teach us Your way, come lead us.

Come, Holy Spirit.
Come, Holy Spirit.

21

COME INTO THE HEAVENLIES
And sing the song the angels sing,
Worthy, worthy.
Come into the heavenlies
And sing the song of the redeemed,
Worthy, worthy.

Worthy is the Lamb.
Worthy is the Lamb.
Worthy is the Lamb.
Worthy is the Lamb.

Worthy of blessing and honour,
Worthy of glory and power,
Worthy is the Lamb.
(Repeat)

22

(Men)   **COME LET US RETURN** unto the
             Lord.
(Women) Come let us return unto the Lord.
(Men)   Come let us return unto the Lord.
(Women) Come let us return unto the Lord.
                                  (Repeat)

For He has torn us,
But He will heal us.
For He has wounded us,
But He will bandage us.
And He will come,
He'll come to us like rain, spring rain.
He will come to us like rain, spring rain.

23

COME, LET US WORSHIP JESUS,
King of nations, Lord of all.
Magnificent and glorious,
Just and merciful.

Jesus, King of the nations,
Jesus, Lord of all.
Jesus, King of the nations,
Lord of all.

Lavish our hearts' affection,
Deepest love and highest praise.
Voice, race and language blending
All the world amazed.

Bring tributes from the nations,
Come in joyful calvacades,
One thunderous acclamation,
One banner raised.

Come, Lord, and fill Your temple,
Glorify Your dwelling place,
Till nations see Your splendour
And seek Your face.

Fear God and give Him glory,
For His hour of judgement comes.
Creator, Lord Almighty,
Worship Him alone.

24 John Pantry.
Copyright © 1993 Kingsway's Thankyou Music.

(Men) **COME, MY SOUL, AND PRAISE THE LORD.** *(Women echo)*
(Men) Sing to Christ, the living Word. *(Women echo)*
(Men) Who heals my broken heart, *(Women echo)*
(Men) And binds my wounds. *(Women echo)*

As His eye is on the sparrow,
So His thoughts are for my life.
Not a moment passes by
But He thinks of me,
And He hears me when I cry.

(Men) Holy, holy is the Lord, *(Women echo)*
(Men) Who may stand before His word? *(Women echo)*
(Men) He knows my life so well, *(Women echo)*
(Men) Yet He loves me still. *(Women echo)*

25 Robert Critchley.
Copyright © 1992 Kingsway's Thankyou Music.

DEEP CALLS TO DEEP
At the sound of Your waterfall,
Touching the deepest part of me.
There is life changing grace
Flowing freely in this place
As Your deep calls to deep in me.

Search me and try me, O God,
For wholly Yours I long to be.
Completely filled and moved
By the power of Your love,
Let Your deep call to deep,
Let Your deep call to deep,
Let Your deep call to deep in me.

26 Ian Smale.
Copyright © 1987 Kingsway's Thankyou Music.

DON'T BE LAZY,
Lazy, lazy, lazy,
But copy those who through faith and patience
Receive what God has promised.

27 Tim & Carla White.
Copyright © 1990 Mercy Publishing/
Kingsway's Thankyou Music.

EVERY TIME I THINK OF YOU
I feel so good inside.
Sometimes words just can't explain
All of the reasons why.
Oh, I never ever want to fall away from You,
So there's one thing I know that I'm gonna do:

I'm never ever ever ever
Ever ever ever gonna stop loving You.
I'm never ever ever ever
Ever ever ever gonna stop loving You.

Your love never lets me down,
Because Your love is true.
And with Your help I know for sure
I'll always be next to You.
Oh, I never ever want to fall away from you,
So there's one thing I know that I'm gonna do:

28 Chris Bowater.
Copyright © 1991 Sovereign Lifestyle Music.

FAITHFUL GOD, faithful God,
All sufficient One, I worship You.
Shalom my peace,
My strong Deliverer,
I lift You up, faithful God.

29

FATHER, I COME TO YOU, lifting up my
    hands
In the name of Jesus, by Your grace I stand.
Just because You love me and I love Your
    Son,
I know Your favour, unending love.

    Unending love,
    Your unending love.

I receive Your favour, your unending love,
Not because I've earned it, not for what I've
    done,
Just because You love me and I love Your
    Son,
I know Your favour, unending love.

It's the presence of Your kingdom as Your
    glory fills this place,
And I see how much You love me as I look
    into Your face.
Nothing could be better, there's nothing I
    would trade
For Your favour, unending love.

30

5000+ HUNGRY FOLK,
5000+ hungry folk,
5000+ hungry folk
Came 4 2 listen 2 Jesus.

The 6 x 2 said O O O,
The 6 x 2 said O O O,
The 6 x 2 said O O O,
Where can I get some food from?

Just 1 had 1 2 3 4 5,
Just 1 had 1 2 3 4 5,
Just 1 had 1 2 3 4 5,
Loaves and 1 2 fishes.

When Jesus blessed the 5 + 2,
When Jesus blessed the 5 + 2,
When Jesus blessed the 5 + 2,
They were increased many x over.

5000+ 8 it up,
5000+ 8 it up,
5000+ 8 it up,
With 1 2 3 4 5 6 7 8 9 10 11 12 basketfuls left
    over.

31

FOCUS MY EYES on You, O Lord,
Focus my eyes on You;
To worship in spirit and in truth,
Focus my eyes on You.

Turn round my life to You, O Lord,
Turn round my life to You;
To know from this night You've made me
    new,
Turn round my life to You.

Fill up my heart with praise, O Lord,
Fill up my heart with praise;
To speak of Your love in every place,
Fill up my heart with praise.

32

FOR THE SAKE OF THE MULTITUDES,
In the power of Jesus Christ,
We are eager to preach the truth,
And to willingly give our lives.
And we know the Shepherd of our souls is
    marching on,
And by His grace we're following His call.

    We hear the cry of the cities,
    We will lift our hearts to God;
    Called and sent in His wonderful love,
    And soul by soul establishing the
        kingdom of God.

33

FROM YOUR THRONE, O LORD let Your fire
    fall upon us;
Let us feel the touch of the Spirit in our
    hearts.
To equip us and empower us, send us out
    to heal the land,
In Your name to shine the light of Christ.

From the Father's heart send us waves of
    Your compassion;
Move us, Lord, to pray for Your will to come
    on earth.
Interceding for a nation that is dying, lost
    and blind,
Let us see them with the eyes of Christ.

Lord, we lift one voice in a song of joy and
   triumph;
Let Your word rise up from our lips, that in
   our lives
We will let the world know Jesus is the
   Victor and the King,
Let our anthem ring throughout the land.

34 Dave Bilbrough.
Copyright © 1994 Kingsway's Thankyou Music.

GIVE YOUR THANKS TO THE RISEN SON.
(Leader - all echo)
To the holy and anointed one. *(echo)*
Who fills our hearts with a joyful song.
   (echo)
Jesus. *(echo)*

Turn to Him, don't be afraid.
Give Him honour, give Him praise.
Lift Him up to the highest place.
Jesus.

(All)
Worship Him, crown Him King,
And give Him all your heart.
(Repeat)

35 Linda Barnhill.
Copyright © 1992 Mercy Publishing/
Kingsway's Thankyou Music.

GLORIFY Your name.
Glorify Your name.
Raise the banner,
Raise it high.
Father, glorify.

Jesus, light the flame.
Jesus, light the flame.
Give us passion
For Your name,
Jesus, light the flame.

Purify Your bride.
Purify Your bride.
Cleanse her with
Your holy fire,
Jesus, purify.

36 Kevin Prosch.
Copyright © 1990 Mercy Publishing/
Kingsway's Thankyou Music.

(And) **GOD IS SO GOOD**
(And) God is so good.

He rides upon the wings of the wind,
He is exalted by His name Jah.
He walks in the midst of the stones of fire,
To be His sons is our desire.
For the natural things speak of the invisible.
Look around and see,
Who could deny the wonders of His love?

You reign on high in majesty,
And the widow's heart causes to sing.
You hear the cry of the fatherless,
And the depths of Your love who can
   comprehend?
For the natural things speak of the invisible.
Look around and see,
Who could deny the wonders of His love?

37 Stuart Townend.
Copyright © 1992 Kingsway's Thankyou Music.

GOD OF HEAVEN, with the heart of a lover;
Conquering King, with compassion in His
   voice.
Sovereign Lord, with the care of a mother;
To You we bring our lives, knowing You will
   take us in.

Jesus Christ, You're the Alpha and Omega:
King of kings, who laid aside His crown.
Man of woes, but a Friend to the friendless:
To You we bring our fears, knowing You
   will set us free.

   *So let's be pure and holy, set apart for
      Jesus;*
   *A covenant people, who reflect the heart
      of God.*
   *With outstretched hands of mercy to the
      broken-hearted,*
   *A covenant people who reveal the love
      of God.*

38 Rosie Fellingham.
Copyright © 1983 Kingsway's Thankyou Music.

GOD, OUR GOD, BLESSES US,
God blesses us,
That all the ends of the earth may fear Him.
(Repeat)

Let all the peoples praise Thee, O God,
Let all the peoples praise Him.

39

GOD, YOU ARE AN AWESOME GOD,
And Your dominion reaches to the heavens;
And all nations sing Your praise,
As Your people we declare Your holiness.

Holy, holy, holy is the Lord
Holy, holy, holy is the Lord.

40

GOLIATH, *thump, thump:* *(x 2)*

"Who will come and fight,
Come on out, you Israelites.
Choose a man to fight,
Come on Israelites!"

David heard him brag,
Put five stones into his bag.
Ran to fight, his face defiant,
He would face the giant.

"Am I a dog?" Goliath asked,
"That you'd choose rocks
To perform your task?
Would you like to be bird feed?
I'll make you the seed."

David said, with twirling sling,
"You forget one little thing:
Battles aren't won with spears and swords,
The battle is the Lord's."

One smooth stone from a little creek bed
Hit Goliath in the head:
There no more giant to dread,
Goliath now was dead.

41

GO TO ALL NATIONS, making disciples,
Baptising them in My name.
Go to all nations, making disciples,
Baptising them in My name.

I am coming soon.
I am coming soon.
I'm waiting at the gates for the Father's
*   call.*
I am coming soon.
Yes I am coming soon.

Teach them to do all I told you to do,
Teach them to walk in My ways.
I have authority in heaven and earth,
I will be with you always.

42

GREAT IS THE DARKNESS that covers the
    earth,
Oppression, injustice and pain.
Nations are slipping in hopeless despair
Though many have come in Your name.
Watching while sanity dies,
Touched by the madness and lies.

Come Lord Jesus, come Lord Jesus,
Pour out Your Spirit we pray.
Come Lord Jesus, come Lord Jesus,
Pour out Your Spirit on us today.

May now Your church rise with power and
    love,
This glorious gospel proclaim.
In every nation salvation will come
To those who believe in Your name.
Help us bring light to this world
That we might speed Your return.

Great celebrations on that final day
When out of the heavens You come.
Darkness will vanish, all sorrow will end,
And rulers will bow at Your throne.
Our great commission complete,
Then face to face we shall meet.

43

HANG ON, stand still, stay put, hold tight;
Wait for the Spirit of God.
Don't push, don't shove, don't move, that's
    right;
Just wait for the Spirit of God.
(Repeat)

For you will receive the power of God,
You will receive the power of God,
You will receive the power of God
When the Holy Spirit comes upon you.

Let's go, launch out, press on, don't fight;
Be filled with the Spirit of God.
Move on, make way, step out, that's right;
Be filled with the Spirit of God.
(Repeat)

For you have received the power of God,
You have received the power of God,
You have received the power of God
Now the Holy Spirit lives within you.

44
Mick Gisbey.
Copyright © 1985 Kingsway's Thankyou Music.

HAVE YOU GOT AN APPETITE?
Do you eat what is right?
Are you feeding on the word of God?
Are you fat or are you thin?
Are you really full within?
Do you find your strength in Him or are you
    starving?

You and me all should be exercising
    regularly,
Standing strong all day long,
Giving God the glory.
Feeding on the living Bread,
Not eating crumbs but loaves instead;
Standing stronger, living longer,
Giving God the glory.

If it's milk or meat you need,
Why not have a slap-up feed,
And stop looking like a weed and start to
    grow?
Take the full of fitness food,
Taste and see that God is good,
Come on, feed on what you should and be
    healthy.

45
David Fellingham.
Copyright © 1992 Kingsway's Thankyou Music.

HE HAS BEEN GIVEN a name above all
    names,
In earth and heaven, let all creation claim
That Jesus Christ is King, and Lord of all.
He is the victor over satan's reign,
His blood has triumphed over sin and
    shame,
Jesus Christ is King and Lord of all.

He is the likeness of Jehovah,
Through whom the world was made.
By His word the universe is sustained,
Every power is subject to His name.

The name of Jesus in victory will resound,
In every nation let the good news sound:
Jesus Christ is King, and Lord of all.

46
Gerald Coates, Noel & Tricia Richards.
Copyright © 1993 Kingsway's Thankyou Music.

HE HAS RISEN,
He has risen,
He has risen,
Jesus is alive.

When the life flowed from His body,
Seemed like Jesus' mission failed.
But His sacrifice accomplished,
Victory over sin and hell.

In the grave God did not leave Him,
For His body to decay;
Raised to life, the great awakening,
Satan's power He overcame.

If there were no resurrection,
We ourselves could not be raised;
But the Son of God is living,
So our hope is not in vain.

When the Lord rides out of heaven,
Mighty angels at His side,
They will sound the final trumpet,
From the grave we shall arise.

He has given life immortal,
We shall see Him face to face;
Through eternity we'll praise Him,
Christ, the champion of our faith.

47
Bob Fitts.
Copyright © 1986 C A Music/Word Music (UK)/
CopyCare Ltd.

HE IS LOVELY, *He is holy,*
Gave supremely, that all men may see.
He is gentle, tender-hearted,
Risen Saviour, He is God.

Master, Maker, Life Creator,
Come and dwell in me,
That my heart may know
Your tender mercy.
Shine through me that all may see
Your love so full and free;
And I'll declare Your praise
Through endless ages.

48

HE IS THE LORD and He reigns on high;
He is the Lord,
Spoke into the darkness, created the light.
He is the Lord.
Who is like unto Him, never ending in days;
He is the Lord
And He comes in power when we call on
    His name.
He is the Lord.

Show Your power, O Lord our God,
Show Your power, O Lord our God,
Our God.

Your gospel, O Lord, is the hope for our
    nation;
You are the Lord.
It's the power of God for our salvation.
You are the Lord.
We ask not for riches, but look to the cross;
You are the Lord.
And for our inheritance give us the lost.
You are the Lord.

Send Your power, O Lord our God,
Send Your power, O Lord our God,
Our God.

49

HE MADE THE EARTH, He made the sky,
He made the moon and stars, Jupiter and
    Mars.
He made the sun for everyone,
Our God made them all.
Our God is powerful, powerful,
Our God is great.
Our God is powerful, powerful,
Our God is great.

He made the fish, He made the birds,
Elephants and worms, creeping things that
    squirm.
Mice so small, giraffes so tall;
Our God made them all.
Our God is wonderful, wonderful,
Our God is great.
Our God is wonderful, wonderful,
Our God is great.

He made the boys, he made the girls,
He made our mums and dads, to teach us
    good from bad.
He cares for me, He cares for you;
Our God loves us all.
Our God is beautiful, beautiful,
Our God is great.
Our God is beautiful, beautiful,
Our God is great.

50

HE REIGNS, *He reigns, Jesus reigns,*
He reigns enthroned in majesty.
Shout Your praise, His banners raise,
For Jesus reigns.
Shout hosanna, Jesus reigns.

Our highest praise we bring
To our great eternal King.
His glory fills the skies,
Now from earth let praise arise.

He spoiled the hosts of hell,
And like blazing stars, they fell.
He led them forth in chains
Now our mighty victor reigns!

51

HOLINESS IS YOUR LIFE IN ME,
Making me clean through Your blood.
Holiness is Your fire in me,
Purging my heart like a flood.
I know You are perfect in holiness.
Your life in me, setting me free,
Making me holy.

Only the blood of Jesus covers all of my
    sin.
Only the life of Jesus renews me from
    within.
Your blood is enough, Your mercy
    complete.
Your work of atonement, paid for my
    debts,
Making me holy.
Only the blood of Jesus.

52

HOLY GHOST,
You wonderful Holy Ghost,
A wind blowing strong,
Blowing from heaven.
(repeat)

We have decided to go
All the way with our God.
Revival in the land, that's our goal;
As soldiers in His army
We'll fight with heart and soul.

(chorus last time)
Blood and fire,
We call upon blood and fire,
A wind blowing strong,
Blowing from heaven.
(repeat)

53

HOLY, HOLY, HOLY IS THE LORD.
Holy, holy, holy is the Lord.
And He is precious in God's sight,
So precious in His eyes.

Worthy, worthy, worthy is the Lamb...

Glory, I give glory to the Lamb of God...

54

HOLY IS YOUR NAME,
Yeshua, my Deliverer.
Worthy of all praise,
You everliving God.

Perfect are Your ways,
Jehovah, my Father.
Faithful is Your love,
You gave Yourself for me.

In You I have security;
In You I put my trust.
In You I have confidence,
You meet my every need.

55

HOLY ONE, my life is in Your hand;
My song an offering of my heart,
Redeemed, washed clean,
By faith I stand secure.
In You Jesus I live.

To You the glory,
To You the power,
To You the honour
Forever more.
Your love brings healing,
Your love's eternal,
Your love's the answer,
The hope of the world,
The hope of the world.

56

HOLY SPIRIT, Holy Spirit,
Pour Your power,
Pour Your power on me, on me, on me.

Holy Spirit, Holy Spirit,
Send Your fire, send Your fire,
Pour Your power,
Pour Your power on me, on me, on me.

Holy Spirit, Holy Spirit
Talk to me, talk to me,
Send Your fire...

Holy Spirit, Holy Spirit,
Guide my life, guide my life,
Talk to me...

Holy Spirit, Holy Spirit,
Bring Your healing, bring Your healing,
Guide my life...

Holy Spirit, Holy Spirit,
Set me free, set me free,
Bring Your healing...

57

HOLY SPIRIT, MOVE WITHIN ME,
Holy Spirit, come upon me now.
Holy Spirit, lead me to the secret place of
   prayer,
Manifest the glory of God.
Holy Spirit, You are welcome,
Holy Spirit, we desire You.
Holy Spirit, worship through us,
Let us see the glory of God.

58 John Newton (1725-1807).

HOW SWEET THE NAME OF JESUS SOUNDS
In a believer's ear;
It soothes his sorrows, heals his wounds,
And drives away his fear.

It makes the wounded spirit whole,
And calms the troubled breast;
'Tis manna to the hungry soul
And to the weary, rest.

Dear name, the Rock on which I build,
My shield, and hiding place;
My never failing treasury, filled
With boundless stores of grace.

Jesus, my Shepherd, Saviour, Friend,
My Prophet, Priest, and King;
My Lord, my Life, my Way, my End,
Accept the praise I bring.

59 Dave Bilbrough.
Copyright © 1994 Kingsway's Thankyou Music.

HOW WONDERFUL, *how glorious*
Is the love of God,
Bringing healing, forgiveness,
Wonderful love.

Let celebration echo through this land;
We bring reconciliation,
We bring hope to every man:

We proclaim the kingdom
Of our God is here;
Come and join the heavenly anthem
Ringing loud and ringing clear:

Listen to the music
As His praises fill the air;
With joy and with gladness
Tell the people everywhere:

60 Dave Bilbrough.
Copyright © 1991 Kingsway's Thankyou Music.

I BELIEVE THERE IS A GOD IN HEAVEN
Who paid the price for all my sin;
Shed His blood to open up the way
For me to walk with Him.

Gave His life upon a cross,
Took the punishment for us,
Offered up Himself in love,
Jesus, Jesus.

'It is finished' was His cry;
Not even death could now deny.
The Son of God exalted high,
Jesus, Jesus,
Jesus.

61 David Fellingham.
Copyright © 1993 Kingsway's Thankyou Music.

I BOW DOWN in humble adoration,
Speak Your name with love and devotion,
Jesus, the Lamb sacrificed for me.
I see Your face, Your tender hands scarred
    for me.
I fall at Your feet with songs of praises
    singing;
My joy is complete, You fulfil my longing.
Prophet of God, my Priest and my King,
I worship and adore.
Before the Father's throne You ever
    intercede;
You always hear my prayer, whatever I may
    plead.
You wipe away my tears, You give me
    victory;
By Your blood I am cleansed, I am free.

62 David Baroni.
Copyright © 1992 Pleasant Hill Music/
Diadem Inc./Kingsway's Thankyou Music.

I DELIGHT IN YOU, LORD.
I delight in Your presence.
There's nothing as sweet
As to sit at Your feet,
Nothing that I'd rather do
Than delight myself,
I delight myself in You.

63 Randy & Terry Butler.
Coypright © 1993 Mercy Publishing/
Kingsway's Thankyou Music.

I KNOW A PLACE, a wonderful place,
Where accused and condemned
Find mercy and grace.
Where the wrongs we have done
And the wrongs done to us
Were nailed there with Him (You),
There on the cross.

(Men)   At the cross,
(Women) At the cross,
(All)   He (You) died for our sin.
(Men)   At the cross,
(Women) At the cross,
(All)   He (You) gave us life again.

64

I LOVE YOU, LORD, MY STRENGTH,
For You heard my cry.
You have been my help in trouble.
I've put my trust in You,
My refuge and my hope,
You're the Rock on which I stand.

You're my stronghold,
You're my stronghold,
You're the stronghold of my life.
You're my stronghold,
You're my stronghold,
You're the stronghold of my life.

I love You, Lord, my strength,
You reached down from on high,
And You rescued me from trouble.
You've taken hold of me,
And set me on a rock,
And now this is where I stand.

I love You, Lord, my strength,
There is no other rock,
And now I will not be shaken.
The sea may roar and crash,
The mountains quake and fall,
Ah, but on this Rock I stand.

65

I'M LOOKING UP TO JESUS,
His face is shining beauty.
I'm feeling so unworthy,
Yet His Spirit leads me on.
I'm looking up to Jesus,
His radiance surrounds me.
I feel so pure and clean,
A taste of heaven on earth.
(Last time)
I'm looking up to Jesus.

66

I'M STANDING HERE TO TESTIFY, *(Leader)*
O, the Lord is good. *(All)*
To sing of how He changed my
   heart. *(Leader)*
O, the Lord is good. *(All)*
I was bound by hate and pride, *(Leader)*
O, the Lord is good. *(All)*
Never knowing of His light, *(Leader)*
O, the Lord is good. *(All)*

I did not think I could have peace, *(Leader)*
O, the Lord is good. *(All)*
Trapped inside by fear and shame, *(Leader)*
O, the Lord is good. *(All)*
He wiped away all of my grief, *(Leader)*
O, the Lord is good. *(All)*
When I believed upon His name. *(Leader)*

Come to the light, come as you are,
You can be the friend of God.
Humble yourself, give Him your heart,
He will meet you where you are.

(Last chorus)
Come to the light, come as you are,
Fall on the Rock for wasted years.
He will restore all that was lost,
Surrender now, His power is here.
Clap Your hands, O God.
Clap Your hands, O God.
Clap Your hands, O God.
Clap Your hands, O God.

67

IN EVERY CIRCUMSTANCE of life
You are with me, glorious Father.
And I have put my trust in You,
That I may know the glorious hope
To which I'm called.
And by the power that works in me,
You've raised me up and set me free;
And now in every circumstance
I'll prove Your love without a doubt,
Your joy shall be my strength,
Your joy shall be my strength.

68

IN MYSTERY REIGNING, King over all,
Hear angels proclaiming, Jesus is Lord.
To each generation Your love is the same,
Wonderful Saviour, we worship Your name.

A beauty that's timeless, who can compare?
All earth stands in silence, when You
   appear.
Your kingdom is boundless, Your love
   without end;
Wonder of wonders, this King is my friend!

All power has been given into Your hands.
Through blood and by suffering You now
   command.
And no opposition can stand in Your light.
Crowned King of heaven, we kneel at the
   sight.

69

IN THESE DAYS OF DARKNESS,
Who will bear the light?
In all of this confusion,
Who will rage against the night?
And who will light a beacon
In the face of this dark, dark sky?

Where there is oppression,
Who will raise the flame?
For the sake of all the children,
Who will touch the fields of shame?
And who will light a beacon
In the face of this dark, dark sky,
With a hope that is eternal,
With a love that will never die?

Oh I, I will carry the fire.
Oh I, I will carry the fire.

Who will burn with passion,
Blazing from the heart,
To forge a new tomorrow?
We must tell the world
Of a hope that is eternal,
Of a love that will never die.
And we will light a beacon
In the face of this dark, dark sky.

Oh I, I will carry the fire.
Oh I, I will carry the fire.
I will not rest, I will not tire,
With all my strength I'll carry the fire.
I will not rest, I will not tire,
With all my strength I'll carry the fire.

70

INTO THE DARKNESS of this world,
Into the shadows of the night;
Into this loveless place You came,
Lightened our burdens, eased our pain,
And made these hearts Your home.
Into the darkness once again,
Oh come, Lord Jesus, come.

Come with Your love to make us whole,
Come with Your light to lead us on,
Driving the darkness far from our souls:
Oh come, Lord Jesus, come.

Into the longing of our souls,
Into these heavy hearts of stone,
Shine on us now Your piercing light,
Order our lives and souls aright,
By grace and love unknown,
Until in You our hearts unite,
Oh come, Lord Jesus, come.

O Holy Child, Emmanuel,
Hope of the ages, God with us,
Visit again this broken place,
Till all the earth declares Your praise
And Your great mercies own.
Now let Your love be born in us,
Oh come, Lord Jesus, come.

(Last Chorus)
Come in Your glory, take Your place,
Jesus, the Name above all names,
We long to see You face to face,
Oh come, Lord Jesus, come.

71

I SING A SIMPLE SONG OF LOVE
To my Saviour, to my Jesus.
I'm grateful for the things You've done,
My loving Saviour, oh precious Jesus.
My heart is glad that You've called me Your
own;
There's no place I'd rather be,

(Than) in Your arms of love,
In Your arms of love,
Holding me still,
Holding me near in Your arms of love.

72

I SING PRAISES TO YOUR NAME, O Lord,
Praises to Your name, O Lord,
For Your name is great and greatly to be
praised.
I sing praises to Your name, O Lord,
Praises to Your name, O Lord,
For Your name is great and greatly to be
praised.

I give glory to Your name…

73

I STAND AMAZED when I realise
Your love for me is beyond all measure.
Lord, I can't deny
Your love for me is great.

It's as high, high as the heavens above,
Such is the depth of Your love
Toward those who fear You.
Oh Lord, far as the east is from west,
You have removed my transgressions.
You make my life brand new;
Father, I love You.

Your love is higher, high as the heavens.
Your love is deeper, deeper than the
deepest ocean.
Your love is stronger, stronger than the
powers of darkness.
Your love is sweeter, sweeter than wine.

74 John Bell & Graham Maule.
Copyright © 1988 Wild Goose Publications.

**IT IS GOOD TO GIVE THANKS TO THE
LORD,**
To remember all He has done;
Then God will remember our praises
When He looks with love on His people.

*O give thanks to the Lord,
For His love endures forever.
O give thanks to the Lord,
For the Lord alone is good.*

Our sin is the sin of our fathers,
We have done wrong, we all have been evil;
Like those who once lived in bondage,
We paid no heed to all You had done.

Our fathers forsook Your love,
At the Red Sea they questioned their God;
They fell from their faith in the desert,
And put God to the test in the wilderness.

Time after time He would rescue them,
Yet in malice they dared to defy Him;
Despite this He came to their aid
When He heard their cries of distress.

Save us, O Lord, in Your love;
Bring us back from all that offends You.
Look not alone at our sins,
But remember Your promise of mercy.

Blessed be the Lord God of Israel
Both now and through all eternity;
Let nations and people cry out
And sing Amen! Alleluia!

75 Terry Butler.
Copyright © 1991 Mercy Publishing/
Kingsway's Thankyou Music.

IT IS THE CRY OF MY HEART *to follow
You.
It is the cry of my heart to be close to
You.
It is the cry of my heart to follow
All of the days of my life.*

Teach me Your holy ways, O Lord,
So I can walk in Your truth.
Teach me Your holy ways, O Lord,
And make me wholly devoted to You.

Open my eyes so I can see
The wonderful things that You do.
Open my heart up more and more
And make it wholly devoted to You.

76 Author unknown.

I'VE GOT THE LIFE OF GOD IN ME.
I've got the life of God in me.
I've got His life, His nature and His ability,
I've got the life of God in me.

I've got the word of God in me.
I've got the word of God in me.
I've got His word, His nature and His ability,
I've got the word of God in me.

I've got the joy of God in me.
I've got the joy of God in me.
I've got His joy, His nature and His ability,
I've got the joy of God in me.

I've got the love of God in me.
I've got the love of God in me.
I've got His love, His nature and His ability,
I've got the love of God in me.

77 Ian White.
Copyright © 1987 Little Misty Music/
Kingsway's Thankyou Music.

I WAITED PATIENTLY for the Lord,
He turned and heard my cry.
He lifted me from the pit,
Out from the mud and mire.
He put my feet on a rock,
And gave me a firm place to stand.
He put a new song in my mouth,
A hymn of praise to God,
A hymn of praise to God.

*Many will see, many will fear,
And many will put their trust in the Lord.
Many will see, many will fear,
And many will put their trust in the Lord.*

Blessed is the man who trusts the Lord,
And turns from all the proud;
From all those who have turned aside,
To follow what is false.
Many are the wonders that You have done,
All the things You have planned;
Were I to count they still would be
Too many to declare,
Too many to declare.

78

I WAS MADE TO PRAISE YOU,
I was made to glorify Your name,
In every circumstance,
To find a chance to thank You.
I was made to love You,
I was made to worship at Your feet,
And to obey you,
I was made for You.

I will always praise You,
I will always glorify Your name,
In every circumstance
To find a chance to thank You.
I will always love You,
I will always worship at Your feet,
And I'll obey You Lord,
I was made for You.

79

I WILL BE YOURS,
You will be mine
Together in eternity.
Our hearts of love
Will be entwined,
Together in eternity,
Forever in eternity.

No more tears of pain in our eyes;
No more fear or shame,
For we will be with You,
For we will be with You.

80

I WILL EXTOL THE LORD with all my heart.
I will extol the Lord with all my heart,
For holy and awesome,
For holy and awesome,
For holy and awesome is His name.

Holy and awesome is His name.
Holy and awesome is His name.
And the fear of the Lord
Is the start of wisdom.
Holy and awesome is His name.

Holy and awesome is His name.
Holy and awesome is His name.
Those who follow His ways
Have a good understanding.
Holy and awesome is His name.

Holy and awesome is His name.
Holy and awesome is His name.
And to Him belong eternal praise.
Holy and awesome is His name.
Holy and awesome is His name.
Holy and awesome is His name.

81

I WILL GIVE THANKS TO THE LORD with all
my heart,
I will sing glorious praises to Your name;
I will be glad and exalt in You, my Lord,
Yesterday, today, forever You're the same.

O, Most High,
You who are my stronghold,
When troubles come,
You're my hiding place;
O, Most High,
Those who know You trust You,
You will not forsake the ones
Who seek Your face.

82

I WILL PRAISE YOU,
O Lord, with all of my heart.
I will praise You,
O Lord, with all of my heart.
Before the gods I will sing your praise.
Before the gods I will praise Your name.

The Lord will fulfil His purpose for me.
The Lord will fulfil His purpose for me.
Do not forsake the work of Your hands,
Revive me, Lord.

You have exalted above all things
Your name and Your word.
You have exalted above all things
Your name and Your word.
I called to you, and You answered me.
When I called to You, You made me strong.

For Your love, O Lord, endures forever,
And Your faithfulness is to the clouds.
Do not forsake the work of Your hands,
Revive me, Lord.

83 Ian White.
Copyright © 1987 Little Misty Music/
Kingsway's Thankyou Music.

I WILL PRAISE YOU WITH THE HARP

For Your faithfulness, O my God.
I will sing my praise to You
With the lyre, with the lyre.

O Holy One of Israel,
O Holy One of Israel,
O Holy One of Israel,
My lips will shout for joy,
My lips will shout for joy.

When I sing my praise to You,
When I sing my praise to You,
When I sing my praise to You,
For I have been redeemed,
I have been redeemed!

(I've been redeemed, I've been
redeemed!
I've been redeemed, I've been
redeemed!)

I'll speak of all Your righteous acts,
I'll speak of all Your righteous acts,
I'll speak of all Your righteous acts,
And tell it all day long,
And tell it all day long.

Those who want to harm me
Are put to shame and confused.
I will sing my praise to You
With the lyre, with the lyre.

84 Maggi Dawn.
Coypright © 1993 Kingsway's Thankyou Music.

I WILL WAIT for Your peace to come to me.

I will wait for Your peace to come to me,
And I'll sing in the darkness,
And I'll wait without fear,
And I'll sing in the darkness,
And I'll wait without fear.

85 Ian Smale.
Copyright © 1985 Kingsway's Thankyou Music.

I WILL WAVE MY HANDS in praise and adoration,

I will wave my hands in praise and
adoration,
I will wave my hands in praise and
adoration,
Praise and adoration to the living God.

For He's given me hands that just love
clapping:
One, two, one, two, three,
And He's given me a voice that just loves
shouting
'Hallelujah!'
He's given me feet that just love dancing:
One, two, one, two, three,
And He's put me in a being
That has no trouble seeing
That whatever I am feeling he is worthy to
be praised.

86 Callie Gerbrandt.
Copyright © 1993 Mercy Publishing/
Kingsway's Thankyou Music.

I WORSHIP YOU, O LORD,

In spirit and truth;
I bow my face before Your throne,
I praise You, Lord.

I glorify Your name,
I magnify Your name;
And I exalt You Lord over all,
I praise You, Lord.

87 Andy Thorpe.
Copyright © 1993 Kingsway's Thankyou Music.

JESUS, (Jesus,)

Jesus, (Jesus,)
It's the Name above all names.
(repeat)

And at the name of Jesus
Every knee shall bow,
And every tongue confess He is Lord.

88 Bryn Haworth.
Copyright © 1993 Kingsway's Thankyou Music.

JESUS, Jesus,

Son of God, Son of man,
Friend of sinners, gift of God.
Jesus, Jesus,
Light of life, Lord of all,
Full of grace and truth.

You have come to us,
Your presence has filled this place.
We will draw near to You,
We come, Lord, to seek Your face.

Jesus, Jesus,
My heart aches, my soul waits,
For Your healing, Lord, I pray.
Jesus, Jesus,
Mighty God, holy Child,
Name above all names.

Jesus, Jesus,
Son of God, Son of Man,
My soul thirsts for You.

89

JESUS, FORGIVE ME.
Jesus, free me.
Jesus, touch me.
Jesus, fill me.

*I lift my head, lift my heart,
Lift my soul to You.
I give my life, give myself,
Give it all to You.*

Jesus, teach me.
Jesus, lead me.
Jesus, guide me.
Jesus, use me.

90

JESUS, I AM THIRSTY, won't You come and fill me?
Earthly things have left me dry, only You can satisfy,
All I want is more of You.

*All I want is more of You,
All I want is more of You;
Nothing I desire, Lord, but more of You.*
(Repeat)

91

JESUS IS THE NAME WE HONOUR;
Jesus is the name we praise.
Majestic Name above all other names,
The highest heaven and earth proclaim
That Jesus is our God.

*We will glorify,
We will lift Him high,
We will give Him honour and praise.
We will glorify,
We will lift Him high,
We will give Him honour and praise.*

Jesus is the name we worship;
Jesus is the name we trust.
He is the King above all other kings,
Let all creation stand and sing
That Jesus is our God.

Jesus is the Father's splendour;
Jesus is the Father's joy.
He will return to reign in majesty,
And every eye at last will see
That Jesus is our God.

92

JESUS RESTORE TO US AGAIN
The gospel of Your holy name,
That comes with power, not words alone,
Owned, signed and sealed from heaven's throne;
Spirit and word in one agreed,
The promise to the power wed.

*The word is near, here in our mouths
And in our hearts, the word of faith,
Proclaim it on the Spirit's breath:
Jesus!*

Your word, O Lord, eternal stands,
Fixed and unchanging in the heavens;
The Word made flesh to earth came down
To heal our world with nail pierced hands.
Among us here You lived and breathed,
You are the Message we received.

Spirit of truth, lead us we pray
Into all truth as we obey,
And as God's will we gladly choose
Your ancient power again will prove
Christ's teaching truly comes from God,
He is indeed the Living Word.

Upon the heights of this dark land
With Moses and Elijah stand,
Reveal Your glory once again,
Show us Your face, declare Your name.
Prophets and Law in You complete,
Where promises and power meet.

Grant us in this decisive hour
To know the Scriptures and the power;
The knowledge in experience proved,
The power that moves and works by love.
May word and works join hands as one,
The word go forth, the Spirit come.

93

LET EVERY TRIBE AND EVERY TONGUE
Bring praise to the Lamb,
For He has triumphed over all,
He has triumphed.
With His blood He has redeemed us
Forever to reign with Him in glory, amen.

We sing glory, glory to the Lamb;
Son of God, the Great I AM.
Awesome in splendour, triumphant King,
We give You praise and dominion over
*   all.*

Worthy, worthy is the Lamb;
Holy, resurrected Lamb.
Jesus, King Jesus, pre-eminent God,
We give You praise,
We give You praise over all.

94

LET'S JOIN TOGETHER,
Lift up our hearts as one;
Let's proclaim His mighty name,
For he has overcome
All that stands before Him
By the power of His blood,
Sing to Jesus the Saviour,
He's the Lord of heaven above.

Come on and dance and sing,
Give Him your everything;
Come on and dance and sing,
He is the Lord.
(Repeat)

He reigns forever,
He is the King of kings,
Our Saviour and Deliverer,
The reason that we sing.
His grace is like a fountain,
A never ending stream;
Let's celebrate together,
And let His praise begin.

Dance now before Him,
Proclaim His victory;
Hail Him as the Saviour
Who's come to set men free.
His word will stand forever,
For all authority
Has been given to Jesus
Through all eternity.

95

LET THE RIGHTEOUS SING,
Come let the righteous dance,
Rejoice before your God,
Be happy and joyful,
Give Him your praise.
We give You our praise.

He gives the desolate a home,
He leads the prisoners out with singing.
Father to the fatherless,
Defender of the widow
Is God in His holy place.

So let the righteous sing…

96

LET US DRAW NEAR to God
In full assurance of faith,
Knowing that as we draw near to Him,
He will draw near to us.
In the holy place
We stand in confidence,
Knowing our lives are cleansed
In the blood of the Lamb,
We will worship and adore.

97

LET YOUR WORD run freely through this
    nation,
Strong Deliverer, break the grip of Satan's
    power.
Let the cross of Jesus stand above the idols
    of this land,
Let anointed lives rise up and take their
    stand.

And we will glorify the Lamb,
Slain from eternity.
Jesus is Lord, we declare His name,
And stand in His victory,
And stand in His victory.

With prophetic words of power expose the
    darkness;
With apostolic wisdom build the church.
With zeal for the lost let the story be told,
Let the shepherds feed the lambs within the
    fold.

Let the Holy Spirit's fire burn within us,
Cleansed from sin and pure within we stand
   upright.
Not yielding to wrong, we will live in
   holiness,
Bringing glory to the Saviour, we will shine.

98 Dave Bilbrough.
Copyright © 1993 Kingsway's Thankyou Music.

LIFT HIM UP, *lift Him high,*
Let His praises fill the sky.
Oh, heaven's gates are open wide
To those who hear the call.
(Repeat)

Through every generation
This truth will always shine,
That Christ came down among us,
Now He is glorified.

The message of the kingdom
Stands unshakeable through time;
That man can be forgiven,
If you seek then you will find.

99 Brian Doerksen.
Copyright © 1992 Mercy Publishing/
Kingsway's Thankyou Music.

LORD, I HAVE HEARD OF YOUR FAME,
I stand in awe of Your deeds, O Lord.
I have heard of Your fame,
I stand in awe of Your deeds, O Lord.

Renew them, renew them,
In our day, and in our time
Make them known.
Renew them, renew them,
In our day, and in our time
Make them known.
In wrath remember mercy.

100 Rick Founds.
Copyright © 1989 Maranatha! Music/
CopyCare Ltd.

LORD, I LIFT YOUR NAME ON HIGH;
Lord, I love to sing Your praises.
I'm so glad You're in my life;
I'm so glad you came to save us.

   You came from heaven to earth
   To show the way.
   From the earth to the cross,
   My debt to pay.
   From the cross to the grave,
   From the grave to the sky,
   Lord, I lift Your name on high.

101 Bev Gammon.
Copyright © 1989 Kingsway's
Thankyou Music.

LORD JESUS, YOU ARE FAITHFUL,
Always with us, never leaving us,
Lord Jesus.

Lord Jesus, You are blameless,
You are perfect, You are sinless,
Lord Jesus.

Lord Jesus, You are so pure,
Pure and lovely, pure and holy,
Lord Jesus.

102 Rick Founds.
Copyright © 1989 Maranatha! Music/
CopyCare Ltd.

LORD, LOOK UPON MY NEED,
I need You, I need You.
Lord, have mercy now on me,
Forgive me, O Lord, forgive me,
And I will be clean.

   O Lord, You are familiar with my ways,
   There is nothing hid from You.
   O Lord, You know the number of my
      days,
   I want to live my life for You.

103 Joe King.
Copyright © 1990 Kingsway's
Thankyou Music.

LORD OF ALL CREATION,
Let this generation
See a visitation of Your power;
Put to flight all the powers of darkness,
O come, Lord Jesus, come.

   Lord of all creation,
   Let this generation
   See a visitation of Your power.
   Lord of all creation,
   There's an expectation
   Rising in this nation every hour.

Father God, forgive us,
Send Your cleansing rivers,
Wash us now and give us holy power;
Fill this land with Your awesome presence,
O come, Lord Jesus, come.

104 Dave Bilbrough.
Copyright © 1993 Kingsway's
Thankyou Music.

LORD, WE COME IN ADORATION,
Lay our lives before You now.
We are here to reach the nations,
To tell the world of Jesus' power.
We would seek Your awesome glory,
All the gifts that you endow.
Called to reach this generation.
And now is the appointed hour.

We will go in Your name;
Go and proclaim Your kingdom.
Go in Your name,
For we have been chosen to tell all
*   creation*
That Jesus is King of all kings.

We believe that You have spoken
Through Your Son to all the earth.
Given us this great commission
To spread the news of all Your worth.
Set apart to serve You only,
Let our lives display Your love;
Hearts infused that tell the story
Of God come down from heaven above.

Grant to us a fresh anointing,
Holy Spirit, be our guide;
Satisfy our deepest longing -
Jesus Christ be glorified.
Every tribe and every people,
Hear the message that we bring;
Christ has triumphed over evil,
Bow the knee and worship Him.

105 Simon & Lorraine Fenner.
Copyright © 1989 Kingsway's
Thankyou Music.

LORD YOU ARE CALLING
The people of Your kingdom,
To battle in Your name against the enemy.
To stand before You,
A people who will serve You,
Till Your kingdom is released
Throughout the earth.

Let Your kingdom come,
Let Your will be done
On earth as it is in heaven.
(Repeat)

At the name of Jesus
Every knee must bow.
The darkness of this age must flee away.
Release Your power
To flow throughout the land,
Let Your glory be revealed
As we praise.

106 David Baroni.
Copyright © 1992 Pleasant Hill Music/
Diadem Inc./Kingsway's Thankyou Music.

LORD, YOU ARE WORTHY,
Lord, You are worthy,
Lord, You are worthy,
We give You praise.

Lord, You are worthy…

Lord, You are holy…

Lord, we adore You…

Lord, You are worthy…

(to end, repeat last line twice)

107 Martin J. Smith.
Copyright © 1992 Kingsway's
Thankyou Music.

LORD, YOU HAVE MY HEART,
And I will search for Yours;
Jesus, take my life and lead me on.
Lord, You have my heart,
And I will search for Yours;
Let me be to You a sacrifice.

And I will praise You, Lord. (Men)
I will praise You, Lord. (Women)
And I will sing of love come down. (Men)
I will sing of love come down. (Women)
And as You show Your face, (Men)
Show Your face, (Women)
We'll see Your glory here. (All)

108 Ian White.
Copyright © 1987 Little Misty Music/
Kingsway's Thankyou Music.

MAY GOD BE GRACIOUS TO US and bless
us,
Make His face to shine upon us.
May Your ways be known over the earth
And Your salvation among all nations.

May the peoples praise You;
O God, may all the peoples praise You.
May the peoples praise You;
O God, may all the peoples praise You.

May the nations be glad and sing for joy,
For with justice You rule the people You
guide.
May Your ways be known over the earth,
And Your salvation among all nations.

Then the harvest will come to the land,
And God, our God, will bless us.
God will bless us, and all the ends
Of earth will fear Him.

109 Chris Bowater.
Copyright © 1992 Sovereign Lifestyle Music.

MAY OUR WORSHIP be as fragrance,
May our worship be as incense poured
    forth,
May our worship be acceptable
As a living sacrifice,
As a living sacrifice.

We are willing to pay the price,
We are willing to lay down our lives
As an offering of obedience,
As a living sacrifice,
As a living sacrifice.

110 Chris A. Bowater/Mark & Helen Johnson.
Copyright © 1991 Sovereign Lifestyle Music.

MIGHTY GOD,
Everlasting Father,
Wonderful Counsellor,
You're the Prince of Peace.

You are the Lord of heaven,
You are called Emmanuel;
God is now with us,
Ever present to deliver.
You are God eternal,
You are the Lord of all the earth;
Love has come to us,
Bringing us new birth.

A light to those in darkness,
And a guide to paths of peace;
Love and mercy dawns,
Grace, forgiveness and salvation.
Light for revelation,
Glory to Your people;
Son of the Most High,
God's love gift to all.

111 Steve & Vikki Cook.
Copyright © 1991 People of Destiny
International/Word Music/Word Music (UK)/
CopyCare Ltd.

MOST HOLY JUDGE, I stood before You
    guilty,
When You sent Jesus to the cross for my
    sin.
There Your love was revealed,
Your justice vindicated,
One sacrifice has paid the cost
For all who trust in Jesus.

Now I'm justified, You declare me
    righteous,
Justified by the blood of the Lamb.
Justified freely by Your mercy,
By faith I stand and I'm justified.

I come to You, and I can call You 'Father',
There is no fear, there is no shame before
    You.
For by Your gift of grace
Now I am one of Your children,
An heir with those who bear Your name,
And share the hope of glory.

112 Trad. (Hindustani)

MUKTI DILAYE Yesu naam,
Shanti dilaye Yesu naam.
(Repeat)
    [Peace comes to you in Jesus' name,
        Salvation in no other name.]

Yesu daya ka behta sagar
Yesu daya ka behta sagar
Yesu hai data mahan
Yesu hai data mahan
    [Jesus is the Ocean of Grace:
        You are majestic, Lord.]

Charni main tooney janam liya Yesu
Charni main tooney janam liya Yesu
Sooley pay kiya vishram
Sooley pay kiya vishram
    [Jesus, You were born in a manger
        (Made of wood):
        You were crucified on the cross
        (Made of wood).]

Peace comes to you in Jesus' name,
Salvation in no other name.

Ham sab key papon ko mitane
Ham sab key papon ko mitane
Yesu hua hai balidan
Yesu hua hai balidan
    [For the remission of our sins,
    Jesus has been sacrificed on the cross.]

Krus par apna khoon bahaa kar
Krus par apna khoon bahaa kar
Sara chukaya daam
Sara chukaya daam
    [By shedding Your blood on the cross,
        You paid the full price for our sins.]

113 Author unknown.

MY GOD IS SO BIG, so strong and so
  mighty,
There's nothing that He cannot do.
My God is so big, so strong and so mighty,
There's nothing that He cannot do.
The rivers are His, the mountains are His,
The stars are His handiwork too.
My God is so big, so strong and so mighty,
There's nothing that He cannot do.

My God is so big, so strong and so mighty,
There's nothing that He cannot do.
My God is so big, so strong and so mighty,
There's nothing that He cannot do.
He's called you to live for Him every day,
In all that you say and you do.
My God is so big, so strong and so mighty,
There's nothing that He cannot do.

114 Chris Williams.
Copyright © 1993 Kingsway's
Thankyou Music.

MY HEART,
I want to give You my heart,
In service to the Lord, the One who cares
To ask for my life.
Take me,
Mould my life and make me
Into a child who longs to stay by Your side
And learn of Your ways.

For when I sought You, Lord, You heard me,
You delivered me from fear;
And by Your grace and mercy
You have brought us both so near.
I want to kneel before Your feet, Lord,
And to gaze upon Your face;
For the God who asks for my life
Loves me completely and always.

115 Graham Kendrick.
Copyright © 1991 Make Way Music.

MY HEART IS FULL of admiration
For You, my Lord, my God and King.
Your excellence my inspiration,
Your words of grace have made my spirit
  sing.

  All the glory, honour and power
  Belong to You, belong to You.
  Jesus, Saviour, Anointed One,
  I worship You, I worship You.

You love what's right and hate what's evil,
Therefore Your God sets You on high,
And on Your head pours oil of gladness,
While fragrance fills Your royal palaces.

Your throne, O God, will last forever,
Justice will be Your royal decree.
In majesty, ride out victorious,
For righteousness, truth and humility.

116 Edward Mote (1797-1854).

MY HOPE IS BUILT on nothing less
Than Jesus' blood and righteousness.
I dare not trust the sweetest frame,
But wholly lean on Jesus' name.

When darkness veils His lovely face
I rest on His unchanging grace.
In every high and stormy gale
My anchor holds within the veil.

  On Christ the solid rock I stand,
  All other ground is sinking sand,
  All other ground is sinking sand.

His oath, His covenant, His blood
Supports me in the 'whelming flood.
When all around my soul gives way,
He then is all my hope and stay.

When He shall come with trumpet sound,
O may I then in Him be found.
Dressed in His righteousness alone,
Faultless to stand before the throne.

117 Noel Richards.
Copyright © 1991 Kingsway's
Thankyou Music.

  MY LIPS SHALL PRAISE YOU,
  My great Redeemer;
  My heart will worship
  Almighty Saviour.

You take all my guilt away,
Turn the darkest night to brightest day,
You are the restorer of my soul.

Love that conquers every fear,
In the midst of trouble You draw near,
You are the restorer of my soul.

You're the source of happiness,
Bringing peace when I am in distress,
You are the restorer of my soul.

118

NEVER LET MY HEART GROW COLD.
Lord, help me to love You
With a love that never dies.
Set my heart ablaze with a burning desire
To see Jesus glorified,
To see Jesus glorified.

119

NEW COVENANT PEOPLE rejoice,
Lift up your eyes and see your King.
Reigning in power on His heavenly throne,
Angels are joyfully singing:

To the Father, our Creator,
To our Judge and Lord.
And to Jesus, Mediator,
Who has cleansed us in His blood.

Let us through Jesus draw near to God,
Offering up our sacrifice,
Confessing that Jesus is Lord over all,
Joining with heavenly praises:

We give thanks to You with fear,
Holy God, consuming fire,
Secure in Your grace we will never be
    moved,
We bring our love and devotion:

120

NO EYE HAS SEEN, no ear has heard,
No mind has conceived what the Lord has
    prepared;
But by His Spirit, He has revealed
His plan to those who love Him.
(Repeat)

We've been held by His everlasting love,
Led with loving kindness by His hand;
We have hope for the future yet to come,
In time we'll understand the mystery of His
    plan.

121

NO OTHER NAME but the name of Jesus,
No other name but the name of the Lord;
No other name but the name of Jesus
Is worthy of glory, and worthy of honour,
And worthy of power and all praise.

His name is exalted far above the earth.
His name is high above the heavens;
His name is exalted far above the earth,
Give glory and honour and praise unto His
    name.

122

NOTHING SHALL SEPARATE US
From the love of God.
Nothing shall separate us
From the love of God.

God did not spare His only Son,
Gave Him to save us all.
Sin's price was met by Jesus' death
And heaven's mercy falls.

Up from the grave Jesus was raised
To sit at God's right hand;
Pleading our cause in heaven's courts,
Forgiven we can stand.

Now by God's grace we have embraced
A life set free from sin;
We shall deny all that destroys
Our union with Him.

123

O FATHER OF THE FATHERLESS,
In whom all families are blessed,
I love the way You father me.
You gave me life, forgave the past,
Now in Your arms I'm safe at last,
I love the way You father me.

Father me, forever You'll father me,
And in Your embrace I'll be forever
    secure.
I love the way You father me.
I love the way You father me.

When bruised and broken I draw near
You hold me close and dry my tears,
I love the way You father me.
At last my fearful heart is still,
Surrendered to Your perfect will,
I love the way You father me.

If in my foolishness I stray,
Returning empty and ashamed,
I love the way You father me.
Exchanging for my wretchedness
Your radiant robes of righteousness,
I love the way You father me.

And when I look into Your eyes
From deep within my spirit cries,
I love the way You father me.
Before such love I stand amazed
And ever will through endless days,
I love the way You father me.

124

O GOD, BE MY STRENGTH
Through my doubt and my fear.
O God, be my comfort
When darkness is near.
O Lord of all hope,
You're my Saviour and Guide.
O Lord, have mercy on me.

O God of all mercy
And God of all grace,
Whose infinite gift
Was to die in my place,
Eternal Creator,
Redeemer and Friend,
O Lord, have mercy on me.

O God of all power,
Invisible King,
Restorer of man,
My life I bring.
O Lord of my heart,
Grant Your peace now I pray,
O Lord, have mercy on me.

125

O GOD, MOST HIGH, Almighty King,
The champion of heaven, Lord of
    everything;
You've fought, You've won, death's lost its
    sting,
And standing in Your victory we sing.

*You have broken the chains
That held our captive souls.
You have broken the chains
And used them on Your foes.
All Your enemies are bound,
They tremble at the sound of Your
    name;
Jesus, You have broken the chains.*

The power of hell has been undone,
Captivity held captive by the Risen One,
And in the name of God's great Son,
We claim the mighty victory You've won.

126

OH, I BELIEVE IN JESUS.
Oh, I believe He's Lord.
Oh, I know he is God's Son.
Oh, I believe His word.

*I'm a believer,
I'm a believer, yeah,
I'm a believer
And I'm never gonna change my mind.*

Oh, I know He's the only One,
Oh, He calls me by my name.
Oh, since the day he touched me,
Oh, I've never been the same.

Jesus died, Jesus paid the price.
He gave me everlasting life.

127

O LAMB OF GOD, You take away our sin.
You clothe us now in robes of
    righteousness.
You set us free and protect us from all
    harm;
In holiness we worship You.

And we will overcome by the blood of the
    Lamb,
As we declare the testimony of the word.
We will overcome by the blood of the Lamb,
As we declare the word of God.

128

O LORD, ARISE, release Your power,
Scatter Your foes this very hour.
May we hold on to Your holy commands.
You are the Lord of every man.

You hold our lives, You give us breath,
You freed us from the power of death.
You're our salvation, our only hope,
You are the Lord of every man.

*Your voice, it is like thunder
Over the waters.
Your voice echoes throughout the earth,
We will bow to the sound,
We will bow to the sound
Of Your voice.*

129

O LORD I WANT TO SING YOUR PRAISES,
I want to praise Your name every day.
O Lord I want to sing Your praises,
I want to praise Your name every day.

> *Alleluia, allelu.*
> *Alleluia, allelu.*
> *(Alleluia.)*

God, You are my God, and I will seek You;
I am satisfied when I find Your love.
God, You are my God, and I will seek You;
I am satisfied when I find Your love.

And I will praise You as long as I live,
For Your love is better than life.
In Your name I will lift up my hands,
For Your love is better than life.

130

O LORD, YOU'RE GREAT, You are fabulous.
We love you more than any words can sing,
    sing, sing.
O Lord, You're great, You are so generous,
You lavish us with gifts when we don't
    deserve a thing.

> *Allelu, alleluia, praise You, Lord.*
> *Alleluia, praise You, Lord.*
> *Alleluia, praise You, Lord.*
> *(Repeat)*

O Lord, You're great, You are so powerful,
You hold the mighty universe in Your hand,
    hand, hand.
O Lord, You're great, You are so beautiful,
You've poured out Your love on this
    undeserving land.

131

ONCE THERE WAS A HOUSE,
A busy little house.
And this is all about
The busy little house.

Jesus Christ had come,
Teaching everyone,
So everyone had run
To the busy little house.

Everyone was there,
You couldn't find a chair,
In fact you had to fight for air
In the busy little house.

A man who couldn't walk,
Was carried to the spot,
But the place was chock-a-block,
In the busy little house.

Whatever shall we do?
Whatever shall we do?
We'll never get him through
Into the busy little house.

We'll open up the roof,
We'll open up the roof,
And then we'll put him through
Into the busy little house.

Then Jesus turned His eyes,
And saw to His surprise
The man coming from the skies
Into the busy little house.

Then Jesus turned and said,
'Get up and take your bed,
And run along instead
From the busy little house.'

132

ONLY ONE THING I ask of the Lord:
Only one thing do I desire:
That I may dwell, may dwell in God's house
All of the days of my life,
All of the days of my life.

Even when days of trouble may come,
I will be safe if God is my home,
For I will hide in the shelter of love
All of the days of my life,
All of the days of my life.

I'll gaze on His beauty,
And sing of His glory;
While I have life within me,
What more could I need?

(Descant)
I'll sing to His holy name,
Forever He is the same,
His faithfulness never change,
Let all of the earth proclaim.

133

O RIGHTEOUS GOD who searches minds
and hearts,
Bring to an end the violence of my foes,
And make the righteous more secure,
O righteous God.

Sing praise to the name of the Lord most
high.
Sing praise to the name of the Lord most
high.
Give thanks to the Lord who rescues me,
O righteous God.

O Lord my God, I take refuge in You;
Save and deliver me from all my foes.
My shield is God the Lord most high,
O Lord my God.

134

O SPIRIT OF GOD, COME DOWN,
Fill this heart of mine.
Let Your power and Your glory shine,
Fill this heart of mine.
Let the rain from heaven fall,
Fill this heart of mine.
Let revival come to us all,
Fill this heart of mine.

And let me worship in reality,
Witness with authority,
Commune with You fervently;
Let Your fire burn in me.
Praying unceasingly.
Let fruitfulness abound in me.
Let Your gifts function powerfully
And let Your fire burn in me,
Let Your fire, let Your fire burn in me.

Burn in holiness and zeal,
Fill this heart of mine.
Let me now Your presence feel,
Fill this heart of mine.
Let the oil of gladness flow,
Fill this heart of mine.
Let the love of Jesus show,
Fill this heart of mine.

135

OUR FATHER IN HEAVEN,
Holy is Your name.
Forgive us our sins, Lord,
As we forgive.
Our Father in heaven
Give us our bread.
Lead us not into temptation,
But deliver us from the evil one.

Your kingdom come, Your will be done.
Your kingdom come, Your will be done.

On the earth as it is in heaven.
Let it be done on the earth.
Amen. Amen.

136

POWER FROM ON HIGH,
Power from on high,
Lord, we are waiting
For power from on high.
Power from on high,
Power from on high,
Lord, we are waiting
For power from on high.

May we taste Your heaven
Here on earth,
May Your Spirit bring us new birth.

May we take Your heaven
To those on earth,
May Your Spirit bring them new birth.

May the truth and the power
Of the life that You give,
Very soon be ours to live.

137

PRAISE AND GLORY,
Wisdom and honour,
Power and strength and thanksgiving
Be to our God forever and ever,
Amen.
(Repeat)

138 Tracy Orrison.
Copyright © 1990 Sound Truth Publishing/
Kingsway's Thankyou Music.

QUIET MY MIND, Lord,
Make me still before You;
Calm my restless heart, Lord,
Make me more like You.
(Repeat)

Raise up my hands that are hanging down;
Strengthen my feeble knees.
May Your love and joy abound,
And fill me with Your peace.

139 John Pantry.
Copyright © 1992 Kingsway's
Thankyou Music.

REJOICE, YOU SONS OF ISRAEL,
God has come to save His people.
What joy, what celebration,
See our Saviour promised long ago.
Poor shepherds stand in awe,
As angel singing fills the air;
And kings come bowing low
To pay their homage there.

> *The light of Israel shall become a fire,*
> *And the Holy One, a flame.*
> *The child of miracles born to be Messiah*
> *Over all the earth will reign.*

See Mary hold her baby,
Son of God in her embrace;
And Joseph stares in wonder
At the look upon the Saviour's face.
Yet who can see the sufferings,
And the victory still to come;
The path that leads to Calvary
Rising up to heaven.

> *(Final chorus)*
> *Hallelujah, hallelujah,*
> *Hallelujah, praise His name.*
> *Hallelujah, hallelujah,*
> *Hallelujah, praise His name.*

140 Peter Arajs.
Copyright © 1994 Kingsway's
Thankyou Music.

RISE UP, *let Your kingdom arise in us;*
We lift our eyes to the skies, and rise up
To the brightness of His rising.
(Repeat)

All creation awaits
The revealing of the sons of God,
And all the angels of heaven
Are listening for the prayers of us:
Hearing the sound of a powerful flood,
Saints of our God who've been bought by
  His blood.

The redemption of God
Has given us a kingdom view,
And His promise to us,
The hope of glory, Christ in you.
Darkness shall run from the strength of His
  hand,
Our testimony, the blood of the Lamb.

141 David Fellingham.
Copyright © 1994 Kingsway's
Thankyou Music.

RUACH, Ruach,
Holy wind of God, blow on me.
Touch the fading embers, breathe on me.
Fan into a flame all that You've placed in
  me;
Let the fire burn more powerfully.
Ruach, Ruach,
Holy wind of God,
Holy wind of God, breathe on me.

142 Adrian Howerd & Pat Turner.
Copyright © 1985 Restoration Music Ltd./
Adm. by Sovereign Music (UK).

SALVATION BELONGS TO OUR GOD,
Who sits on the throne,
And to the Lamb.
Praise and glory, wisdom and thanks,
Honour and power and strength,
Be to our God for ever and ever,
Be to our God for ever and ever,
Be to our God for ever and ever, Amen.

And we, the redeemed shall be strong
In purpose and unity,
Declaring aloud
Praise and glory, wisdom and thanks,
Honour and power and strength,
Be to our God for ever and ever,
Be to our God for ever and ever,
Be to our God for ever and ever, Amen.

143

SAY THE WORD, I will be healed,
You are the great Physician,
You meet every need.
Say the word, I will be free,
Where chains have held me captive,
Come sing Your songs to me,
Say the word.

Say the word, I will be filled,
My hands reach out to heaven,
Where striving is stilled.
Say the word, I will be changed,
Where I am dry and thirsty,
Send cool, refreshing rain,
Say the word.

His tears have fallen like rain on my life,
Each drop a fresh revelation;
I will return to the place of the cross,
Where grace and mercy pour from heaven's
    throne.

Say the word, I will be poor,
That I might know the riches
That You have in store.
Say the word, I will be weak,
Your strength will be the power
That satisfies the meek,
Say the word.

The Lord will see the travail of His soul,
And He and I will be satisfied;
Complete the work You have started in me,
O come Lord Jesus, shake my life again.

144

SEEK RIGHTEOUSNESS, seek humility,
That you may be sheltered on that day.

We are silent before You, O solemn Lord,
For the day You have prepared is near.

    *We seek righteousness, we seek
        humility,*
    That we may be sheltered on that day.
    *We seek righteousness, we seek
        humility,*
    That we may be sheltered on that day.

Seek His face, you humble of the land,
You who do what he commands.

Oh, bitter will be the cry on that day;
A day of anguish and distress.
Oh, bitter will be the cry on that day;
A day of anguish and distress.

145

SEND ME OUT FROM HERE, *Lord,*
To serve a world in need.
*May I know no man by the coat he
    wears,*
But the heart that Jesus sees.
*And may the light of Your face
Shine upon me Lord.*
*You have filled my heart with the
    greatest joy*
And my cup is overflowing.

'Go now, and carry the news
To all creation, every race and tongue.
Take no purse with you,
Take nothing to eat
For He will supply your needs.'

'Go now, bearing the light,
Living for others, fearlessly walking into the
    night;
Take no thought for your lives,
Like lambs among wolves,
Full of the Spirit, ready to die.'

146

SHINING FORTH IS YOUR MERCY,
    O Lord, to the poor,
    The sick are healed and the blind see;
    Proclaiming favour the captives are free,
    *'Cause the Lord pours out His Spirit
        upon our land.*

Let the battle cry resound,
Let the heavens' trumpets sound,
See the kingdom come,
In glory the kingdom comes.
Let the holy banners raise,
Let the army shout in praise,
See the kingdom come,
In glory the kingdom comes.

Coming forth from Your throne
The heavens tremble;
Rising mighty in power,
Great is Your name, O Lord.

147 Andy Park.
Copyright © 1989 Mercy Publishing/
Kingsway's Thankyou Music.

SHOW ME, DEAR LORD, how You see me in
 Your eyes,
So that I can realise Your great love for me.
Teach me, O Lord, that I am precious in
 Your sight,
That as a father loves his child, so You love
 me.

 I am Yours because you have chosen
 me.
 I'm Your child because You've called my
 name,
 And Your steadfast love will never
 change;
 I will always be Your precious child.

Show me, dear Lord, that I can never earn
 Your love,
That a gift cannot be earned, only given.
Teach me, O Lord, that Your love will never
 fade,
That I can never drive away Your great
 mercy.

148 Stuart Garrard.
Copyright © 1994 Kingsway's
Thankyou Music.

SING TO THE LORD with all of your heart;
Sing of the glory that's due to His name.
Sing to the Lord with all of your soul,
Join all of heaven and earth to proclaim:

 You are the Lord, the Saviour of all,
 God of creation, we praise You.
 We sing the songs that awaken the
 dawn,
 God of creation, we praise You.

Sing to the Lord with all of your mind,
With understanding give thanks to the King.
Sing to the Lord with all of your strength,
Living our lives as a praise offering.

149 Dave Bilbrough.
Copyright © 1994 Kingsway's
Thankyou Music.

SOUND THE TRUMPET, strike the drum,
See the King of glory come,
Join the praises rising from
The people of the Lord.
Let your voices now be heard,
Unrestrained and unreserved,
Prepare the way for His return,
You people of the Lord.

Sing Jesus is Lord;
Jesus is Lord.
Bow down to His authority,
For He has slain the enemy.
Of heaven and hell He holds the key.
Jesus is Lord;
Jesus is Lord.

150 Craig Musseau.
Copyright © 1991 Mercy Publishing/
Kingsway's Thankyou Music.

SPEAK NOW, JESUS,
Your servant is listening.
Come now, Jesus,
Reveal Your heart to me.
And I'll still my heart,
And set it apart,
For Your word brings peace
To my wandering soul,
I will wait for You.

151 Dave Browning.
Copyright © 1986 Glory Alleluia Music/
Word (UK)/CopyCare Ltd.

TAKE ME PAST THE OUTER COURTS,
And through the holy place.
Past the brazen altar,
Lord, I want to see Your face.
Pass me by the crowds of people,
And the priests who sing their praise;
I hunger and thirst for Your righteousness,
But it's only found one place,

 So take me into the Holy of holies,
 Take me in by the blood of the Lamb;
 So take me into the Holy of holies,
 Take the coal, cleanse my lips, here I am.

152 Kevin Prosch.
Copyright © 1991 Mercy Publishing/
Kingsway's Thankyou Music.

TEACH US, O LORD, what it really means
To rend our hearts instead of outer things,
And teach us, O Lord, what we do not see
About our hearts and of Your ways.
And Father deal with our carnal desires,
To move in Your power, but not live the life,
And to love our neighbour with all that we
 have,
And keep our tongues from saying things
 we have not seen.

O, break our hearts with the things that
   break Yours,
If we sow in tears we will reap in joy,
That we might pass through Your
   refining fire,
Where brokenness awaits on the other
   side.

Raise up an army like Joel saw,
Your church that is stronger than ever
   before.
They do not break ranks when they plunge
   through defences,
But the fear of the Lord will be their
   wisdom.
That they might weep as Jesus wept,
A fountain of tears for the wounded and
   lost;
Whoever heard of an army of God
That conquered the earth by weeping,
And mourning, and brokenness?

   But there will be a day when the nations
     will bow
   And our Lord will be King over all the
     earth;
   And he will be the only one,
   And also His name will be the only one.

153

THE CRUCIBLE FOR SILVER
And the furnace for gold,
But the Lord tests the heart of this child.
Standing in all purity,
God, our passion is for holiness,
Lead us to the secret place of praise.

   Jesus, Holy One, You are my heart's
     desire.
   King of kings, my everything,
   You've set this heart on fire.
   (Repeat)

Father take this offering,
With our song we humbly praise You.
You have brought Your holy fire to our lips.
Standing in Your beauty, Lord,
Your gift to us is holiness;
Lead us to the place where we can sing:

154

THE LORD FILLS ME WITH HIS STRENGTH,
And protects me wherever I go.
The Lord fills me with His strength,
And protects me wherever I go.

Wherever I go, wherever I go,
The Lord protects me wherever I go.
Wherever I go, wherever I go,
The Lord protects me wherever I go.

155

THE LORD HAS SPOKEN.
              (men/women echo)
His purpose stands.   *(men/women echo)*
The Lord has spoken.
              (men/women echo)
His purpose stands.   *(men/women echo)*

Does God speak and then not act?
Make a vow and not fulfil?
I will choose to serve the Lord
Wholeheartedly, wholeheartedly.

   (Ch 1.)
   Oh, raise up a church with a different
     spirit,
   Like Caleb's spirit, believing Your word.
   Oh, raise up a church who will not sin,
   They press on in to possess the land.

You began with just one man,
A covenant with Abraham.
Promising that through his seed
All the nations would be blessed,
And now Your plan is manifest.

   (Repeat Ch 1.)

   (Ch 2.)
   Oh, raise up a church who will walk by
     faith,
   In the fear of God they overcome.
   Oh, raise up a church whose God is with
     them,
   They walk in wisdom, they fear no harm.

Deliver us from the fear of man,
And by Your grace we shall stand.
We'll call to mind Your mighty works
And Your acts of sovereign power;
We'll gather strength as we agree
The battle belongs to the Lord.

(Repeat Ch 1 & 2.)

(Ch 3.)
Oh, raise up a church who revere Your judgements,
They lift up a banner of mercy and love.
Oh, raise up a church who'll not keep silent,
They speak of the glory of Your dear Son.

156

THE LORD REIGNS, *the Lord reigns,*
The Lord reigns,
Let the earth rejoice, let the earth rejoice,
Let the earth rejoice.
Let the people be glad
That our God reigns.

A fire goes before Him
And burns up all His enemies;
The hills melt like wax
At the presence of the Lord,
At the presence of the Lord.

The heavens declare His righteousness,
The peoples see His glory;
For You, O Lord, are exalted
Over all the earth,
Over all the earth.

157

THE LORD WILL RESCUE ME from every evil attack
And bring me safely to His heavenly kingdom.
The Lord will rescue me from every evil attack
And bring me safely to His heavenly kingdom.
To Him be glory for ever and ever, amen.
To Him be glory for ever and ever, amen.

158

THE PRECIOUS BLOOD OF JESUS,
The only cleansing power.
My guilt and shame are washed away
Beneath its crimson flood.

The precious name of Jesus,
The name by which we're saved.
He bore the cross I should have had,
A ransom for my sin.

And I'm forever grateful,
And I will always trust
The precious blood of Jesus,
The sacrifice of love,
The sacrifice of love.

159

THERE IS A HOME that wanderers seek,
There is a strength that lifts the weak;
There is hope for those that know despair.
There is a cup that satisfies,
There is a friend who dries my eyes;
There is peace for those with heavy hearts.

Tender mercy,
The tender mercy of our God,
From lips of sinners
He has heard the faintest cry.
Tender mercy,
The tender mercy of our God,
He has relented,
And His grace is my delight.

I have resolved to know Him more,
He whom the hosts of heaven adore,
Mighty King, whose reign will never end;
Yet as I gaze at the Holy One,
He beckons me to closer come,
Bares the scars that show to me my worth.

160

THERE IS HOLY GROUND to walk upon,
There is peace that you can know;
Faith in God can fill your heart,
And fear and doubt may go.
There is holy ground to walk upon,
Leave behind your heavy shoes;
Come and stand in the shadow of His hands,
For He is calling You.
Come and stand in the shadow of His hands,
For He is calling You.

There is holy ground to walk upon,
Hear Him beckon to the lame;
For there His healing power may flow,
And limbs find strength again.
There is holy ground to walk upon,
There is holy work to do;
Trusting in the words of life,
That Jesus births in you.
Trusting in the words of life,
That Jesus births in you.

There are holy dreams to dream upon,
Vision from the Lord on high;
Jesus may be showing you,
But will you turn your eyes?
There is holy ground to walk upon,
You can find the Jesus road;
Do not wait another day,
But tell Him you will go.
Do not wait another day,
But tell Him you will go.

161 Lenny LeBlanc.
Copyright © 1991 Integrity's Hosanna! Music/
Adm. by Kingsway's Thankyou Music.

THERE IS NONE LIKE YOU,
No one else can touch my heart like You do.
I could search for all eternity long and find
There is none like You.

Your mercy flows like a river wide,
And healing comes from Your hands.
Suffering children are safe in Your arms;
There is none like You.

162 Eddie Espinosa.
Copyright © Mercy Publishing/
Kingsway's Thankyou Music.

THERE'S NO ONE LIKE YOU, my Lord,
No one could take Your place;
My heart beats to worship You,
I live just to seek Your face.
There's no one like You, my Lord,
No one could take Your place;
There's no one like You, my Lord,
No one like You.

*You are my God. You're everything to
    me,
There's no one like You, my Lord, no one
    like You.
You are my God. You're everything to
    me,
There's no one like You, my Lord,
No one like You.*

There's no one like You, my Lord,
No one could take Your place;
I long for Your presence, Lord,
To serve You is my reward.
There's no one like You, my Lord,
No one could take Your place;
There's no one like You, my Lord,
No one like you.

163 Ian Smale.
Copyright © 1994 Glorie Music/
Kingsway's Thankyou Music.

THERE'S NOTHING I LIKE BETTER
Than to praise.
There's nothing I like better
Than to praise.
'Cause Lord, I love You,
And there's nothing I would rather do
Than whisper about it,
Talk all about it.
Shout all about it all my days.

164 Mick Gisbey.
Copyright © 1985 Kingsway's
Thankyou Music.

THE SKY IS FILLED with the glory of God.
Triumphantly the angels sing:
"Rejoice, good news, a Saviour is born,
And life will never be the same."

*Emmanuel.
Emmanuel.
Emmanuel.*

Praise and adoration spring from our hearts,
We lift our voices unto You;
You are the One, God's only Son,
King of kings forever more!

165 Graham Kendrick.
Copyright © 1985 Kingsway's
Thankyou Music.

THIS IS MY BELOVED SON
Who tasted death
That you, my child, might live.
See the blood He shed for you,
What suffering,
Say what more could He give?
Clothed in His perfection
Bring praise, a fragrance sweet,
Garlanded with joy,
Come worship at His feet,

That the Lamb who was slain
Might receive the reward,
Might receive the reward of His
suffering.

Look, the world's great harvest fields
Are ready now,
And Christ commands us: 'Go!'
Countless souls are dying
So hopelessly,
His wondrous love unknown.
Lord, give us the nations
For the glory of the King.
Father, send more labourers,
The lost to gather in.

Come the day when we will stand
There face to face,
What joy will fill His eyes.
For at last His bride appears,
So beautiful,
Her glory fills the skies.
Drawn from every nation,
People, tribe and tongue;
All creation sings,
The wedding has begun.

And the Lamb who was slain
Shall receive the reward,
Shall receive the reward of His suffering.

166

THIS IS THE MYSTERY,
That Christ has chosen you and me
To be the revelation of His glory;
A chosen, royal, holy people
Set apart and loved,
A bride preparing for her King.

Let the Bride say, 'come,'
Let the Bride say, 'come,'
Let the Bride of the Lamb
Say, 'come Lord Jesus!'
Let the Bride say, 'come,'
Let the Bride say, 'come,'
Let the Bride of the Lamb
Say, 'come Lord Jesus, come!'

She's crowned in splendour
And a royal diadem,
The King is enthralled by her beauty.
Adorned in righteousness,
Arrayed in glorious light,
The Bride in waiting for her King.

Now hear the Bridegroom call,
"Beloved, come aside;
The time of betrothal is at hand.
Lift up your eyes and see
The dawning of the day,
When as King, I'll return to claim My bride."

167

TO BE IN YOUR PRESENCE,
To sit at Your feet,
Where Your love surrounds me,
And makes me complete.

This is my desire, O Lord,
This is my desire.
This is my desire, O Lord,
This is my desire.

To rest in Your presence,
Not rushing away,
To cherish each moment,
Here I would stay.

168

TOUCH MY LIPS with holy fire
From the altar, from the throne.
Touch my lips, purify them,
May my words be as Your own.

Always life-giving,
Thanksgiving, forgiving,
Always believing
And speaking what is good:
And always honouring,
Preferring in love each other,
Love never boasts, it always covers,
Touch my lips.

169

TO YOUR MAJESTY and Your beauty I
surrender.
To Your holiness and Your love I surrender.
For You are an awesome God who is
mighty,
You deserve my deepest praise;
With all of my heart,
With all of my life, I surrender.

170

WE ARE HIS PEOPLE,
He gives us music to sing.
But there is a sound now,
Like the sound of the Lord when His
enemies flee.
But there is cry in our hearts,
Like when deep calls unto the deep,
For Your breath of deliverance,
To breathe on the music we so desperately
need.
But without Your power,
All we have are these simple songs.
If you'd step down from heaven,
Then the gates of hell would surely fall.

Shout to the Lord, shout to the Lord,
Shout to the Lord of hosts.
Shout to the Lord, shout to the Lord,
Shout to the Lord of hosts
And it breaks the heavy yoke, breaks the
heavy yoke
When you shout, you shout to the Lord.
It breaks the heavy yoke, breaks the heavy
yoke
When you shout, you shout to the Lord.

171

WE ARE MARCHING in the light of God,
We are marching in the light of God,
We are marching in the light of God,
We are marching in the light of God.

We are marching, marching,
We are marching, marching,
We are marching in the light of God.
We are marching, marching,
We are marching, marching,
We are marching in the light of God.

Siyahamb' ekukhanyen' kwenkhos',
Siyahamb' ekukhanyen' kwenkhos',
Siyahamb' ekukhanyen' kwenkhos',
Siyahamb' ekukhanyen' kwenkhos'.

Siyahamba, hamba, siyahamba, hamba.
Siyahamb' ekukhanyen' kwenkhos'.
Siyahamba, hamba, siyahamba, hamba.
Siyahamb' ekukhanyen' kwenkhos'.

172

WE ARE THE ARMY OF GOD, sons of
Abraham,
We are a chosen generation.
Under a covenant, washed by His precious
blood,
Filled with the mighty Holy Ghost.

And I hear the sound of the coming rain,
As we sing the praise to the great I AM.
And the sick are healed, and the dead will
rise,
And Your church is the army that was
prophesied.

173

WE CONFESS THE SINS OF OUR NATION,
And, Lord we are guilty of a prayerless life.
We've turned away our hearts from Your
laws,
And have taken for granted Your
unchanging grace.
Turn away this curse from our country;
We say that we've robbed You, and our
storehouses are bare.
Open wide the floodgates of heaven,
Rebuke the devourer so we may not be
destroyed.

You said that if we'd humble ourselves
And begin to pray,
You would heal our barren land,
And cleanse us with Your rain.

Don't pass us by, let this be the generation,
Lord,
That lifts up Your name to all the world.
Save us, O God, save a people for Yourself,
O Lord,
Let the fear of the Lord be a standard.
Save us, O God, cleanse us from our
unfaithfulness,
Let the place where we live be called a
house of prayer.

174

WE GIVE THANKS
To You, O Lord Almighty God;
The One who is,
Who was, and is to come.
You've taken up Your power
And begun to reign;
The nations bow before
The Holy One.

Now Your salvation,
And Your power
And Your kingdom
Have all come,
And You are Lord of all.
The accuser of the brothers
Has been hurled down forever,
Overcome by the blood,
Overcome by Your blood,
Overcome by the blood
Of the Lamb.

175

WE HAVE A VISION for this nation;
We share a dream for this land.
We join with angels in celebration,
By faith we speak revival to this land.

*Where every knee shall bow and worship
You,
And every tongue confess that You are
Lord;
Give us an open heaven, anoint our
prayers this day,
And move Your sovereign hand across
this nation.*

176

WE HAVE CALLED ON YOU, LORD
And You have heard us.
We have called on Your name,
And You have answered.
Mercy has triumphed over judgement.
Mercy has triumphed over judgement.

You have stretched out Your hand
And You have touched us,
Sent us Your holy fire,
And You have purged us.
Light has triumphed over darkness.
Light has triumphed over darkness.

We love You, and sing to You,
God of our salvation.
You've rescued us and we declare
Your glory to the nations.
We give our lives, a living sacrifice,
Empty and ready to be filled
With Your power.

177

WELCOME, KING OF KINGS!
*How great is Your name.
You come in majesty,
Forever to reign.*

You rule the nations,
They shake at the sound of Your name.
To You is given all power,
And You shall reign.

Let all creation bow down
At the sound of Your name.
Let every tongue now confess,
The Lord God reigns.

178

**WE'RE STANDING HERE WITH OPEN
HEARTS,**
Our voices joined in unity.
We know we don't lead perfect lives,
And we cry to You for mercy.
Father in heaven, we honour Your name,
That we might bring You glory and fame;
Pour out Your Spirit upon us we pray,
To heal and deliver and save.

*This is our heart cry;
This is our heart cry.*
(Repeat)

We stand before the throne of grace,
A people for Your possession;
We hunger and thirst, we seek Your face,
Come touch us with Your presence.
Father in heaven, holy and true,
Stretch out Your hand, let power break
through;
Pour out Your Spirit upon us today,
To heal and deliver and save.

179

WE'VE GOT A LOT OF HOPE, *a little
faith,
We've got the power of God
To run the race,
It's great to be the children of the great
King.
We walk tall, we see straight,
We're gonna tell the world,
We won't hesitate,
It's great to be the children of the great
King.*

Sometimes confusion can get in the way.
We know the truth, so who cares what they
  say.
We look high, we look low,
We want to tell everybody what we know:
It's great to be the children of the great
  King.

Don't mind the devil, start shouting Him
  down.
Jesus is Lord and He's wearing the crown.
We look high, we look low,
We want to tell everybody what we know:
It's great to be the children of the great
  King.

180 Doug Horley.
Copyright © 1993 Kingsway's
Thankyou Music.

WE WANT TO SEE JESUS LIFTED HIGH,
A banner that flies across this land,
That all men might see the truth and know
He is the way to heaven.
(Repeat)

We want to see, we want to see,
We want to see Jesus lifted high.
We want to see, we want to see,
We want to see Jesus lifted high.

Step by step we're moving forward,
Little by little taking ground,
Every prayer a powerful weapon,
Strongholds come tumbling down,
And down, and down, and down.

We're gonna see...

181 Dave Bilbrough.
Copyright © 1992 Kingsway's
Thankyou Music.

WE WILL TEAR DOWN EVERY STRONGHOLD
Through the power of His word.
We will seek to bring His kingdom in,
Make a way for His return.

We will tell of His salvation,
For the church of Christ is called
To bring healing to the nations,
See His righteousness restored.

  Satan is defeated,
  Christ has overcome,
  Seated at the Father's hand,
  Lord, on earth may Your will now be
    done.

182 Dennis Jernigan.
Copyright © 1989 Shepherd's Heart Music/
Sovereign Music UK.

WE WILL WORSHIP THE LAMB OF GLORY,
We will worship the King of kings;
We will worship the Lamb of glory,
We will worship the King.

And with our hands lifted high
We will worship and sing,
And with our hands lifted high
We come before You rejoicing.
With our hands lifted high to the sky,
When the world wonders why,
We'll just tell them we're loving our King.
Oh, we'll just tell them we're loving our
  King.
Yes, we'll just tell them loving our King.

Bless the name of the Lamb of glory,
I bless the name of the King of kings;
Bless the name of the Lamb of glory,
Bless the name of the King.

183 Bryn and Sally Haworth.
Copyright © 1983 Signalgrade/
Kingsway's Thankyou Music.

WHAT KIND OF LOVE IS THIS
That gave itself for me;
I am the guilty one, yet I go free.
What kind of love is this,
A love I've never known;
I didn't even know His name,
What kind of love is this?

What kind of man is this,
That died in agony?
He who had done no wrong
Was crucified for me.
What kind of man is this,
Who laid aside His throne
That I may know the love of God?
What kind of man is this?

By grace I have been saved;
It is the gift of God.
He destined me to be His son,
Such is His love.
No eye has ever seen,
No ear has ever heard,
Nor has the heart of man conceived
What kind of love is this.

184 Tommy Walker.
Copyright © 1992 Integrity's Hosanna! Music/
Adm. by Kingsway's Thankyou Music.

WHERE THERE ONCE WAS ONLY HURT,
He gave His healing hand;
Where there once was only pain,
He brought comfort like a friend.
I feel the sweetness of His love
Piercing my darkness.
I see the bright and morning sun
As it ushers in His joyful gladness.

He's turned my mourning into dancing
again,
He's lifted my sorrow.
I can't stay silent,
I must sing for His joy has come.

His anger lasts for a moment in time;
But His favour is here
And will be on me for all my lifetime.

185 Alex Muir.
Copyright © 1993 Kingsway's
Thankyou Music.

WHOSE LIPS WILL PLEAD
For the people of this land?
Who'll stand in the gap,
And who'll build up the wall,
Before the long day of God's patience is
over,
Before the night comes
When His judgement will fall?

And whose eyes will weep
For the people of this land?
And whose hearts will break
For the hearts made of stone,
For those who are walking out into the
darkness,
Away from God's love,
Without Christ, so alone?

And whose ears can hear
What the Spirit is saying
To those who are willing
To watch and to pray?
Pray on 'till God's light
Fills the skies over this land,
The light of revival that brings a new day.

186 Carl Tuttle.
Copyright © 1992 Mercy Publishing/
Kingsway's Thankyou Music.

YET THIS WILL I CALL TO MIND,
And therefore will I hope,
Because of the Lord's great love
I've been redeemed.
The Lord is gracious and kind
To all who call on His name,
Because of the Lord's great love
I've been redeemed.

Because of the Lord's great love,
Because of the Lord's great love,
Because of the Lord's great love,
I've been redeemed.

I know of His steadfast love,
His mercy renewed each day,
Because of the Lord's great love
I've been redeemed.
Washed in the blood of the Lamb,
Guiltless forever I stand,
Because of the Lord's great love
I've been redeemed.

187 Craig Musseau.
Copyright © 1989 Mercy Publishing/
Kingsway's Thankyou Music.

YOU ARE MIGHTY,
You are holy,
You are awesome in Your power.
You have risen,
You have conquered,
You have beaten
The power of death.

Hallelujah, we will rejoice.
Hallelujah, we will rejoice.

188 Brian Doerksen.
Copyright © 1991 Mercy Publishing/
Kingsway's Thankyou Music.

YOU ARE MY KING, (You are my King)
And I love You.
You are my King, (You are my King)
And I worship You.
Kneeling before You now,
All of my life I gladly give to You.
Placing my hopes and dreams
In Your hands,
I give my heart to You.

I love You,
Love You, Jesus.
Yes, I love You,
Love You, Jesus my King.

189

YOU ARE RIGHTEOUS in all Your ways,
You are good, You are good.
You are truthful in all You say,
You are good, You are good.

And I bow my knee before You,
In honour of Your name,
For You alone are worthy,
Worthy of my praise,
Worthy of praise.

You are holy, faithful and true,
You are good, You are good.
You are gracious in all You do,
You are good, You are good.

190

YOU ARE THE GREAT I AM,
Forever You will be.
Let every angel sing
Of Your perfect authority.
Every knee will bow
And every tongue confess;
You are the great I AM,
The first and last.

> *Mighty, (Mighty)*
> *Eternal, (Eternal)*
> *Immortal, (Immortal)*
> *Awesome One, (Awesome One)*
> *Mysterious, (Mysterious)*
> *The Wonderful, (The Wonderful)*
> *The Holy One, (The Holy One)*
> *The Beginning and the End.*

191

**YOU ARE THE ONE AND ONLY
   GOD,** *(Men/Women echo)*
There is no other one but You.
And we declare no other name,
Jesus,
Faithful and true. *(All)*

Into Your presence, Lord we
      come *(Men/Women echo)*
We bow before Your majesty:
We look upon You, Holy One,
Jesus,
Jesus. *(All)*

Be enthroned on our praises,
Be exalted on high.
See the love on our faces,
As we glorify, we glorify
(Repeat)
Your name.

192

YOU ARE WONDERFUL,
Counsellor, Mighty God.
You are Prince of Peace,
Our Father for evermore.
You're the Alpha and Omega,
Lord of all lords.
You are Wonderful,
Counsellor, Mighty God.

193

YOU ARE WORTHY TO RECEIVE
All the honour and praise,
Lamb of God, Prince of Peace,
We lift high Your name.

> *For Yours is the greatness,*
> *The power and the glory;*
> *Lord of the nations,*
> *Have mercy on us.*
> *Though heaven be shaken,*
> *And earth's kingdoms fall,*
> *We will still worship You.*

In the footsteps of our King,
We walk unafraid;
Though the battle may rage,
Our praises will ring.

194

YOU BLESS MY LIFE, and heal me inside,
Over and over again.
You touched my heart
And brought peace of mind,
Over and over again.

> *All I can say is I love You.*
> *All I can say is I need You.*
> *All I can say is I thank You, Lord,*
> *For all that You've done in my life.*

You've been so kind and patient with me,
Over and over again.
When I have strayed You showed me the
way,
Over and over again.

195 Robert Newey.
Copyright © 1990 Kingsway's
Thankyou Music.

YOU CAME to heal the brokenhearted;
You came to make the blind eyes see.
Your light is burning now within us,
As Your word of truth sets us free.

> *And we will fill the earth with the love of*
>   *God*
> *That's been shed abroad in our hearts,*
> *Share with every nation and every land*
> *The grace that He imparts.*
> *And we will sing a new song of joy and*
>   *peace,*
> *A resounding trumpet call,*
> *Causing hearts to rise, opening eyes to*
>   *see*
> *That Jesus, Jesus is Lord of all.*

You come in all Your mighty power,
You come to bring the latter rain,
We know You've filled us with Your Spirit
And a love we cannot contain.

You'll come in glory and splendour,
You'll come to reign upon the earth,
We know we'll live with You forever
And declare Your mighty worth.

196 Mark Altrogge.
Copyright © 1991 People of Destiny
International/Word Music Inc./
Word Music (UK)/CopyCare Ltd.

YOU HAVE BECOME FOR US WISDOM;
You have become for us righteousness.
You have become our salvation;
You have become all our holiness.

> *All that we need is found in You;*
> *Oh, all that we need is in You.*
> *All that we need is found in You;*
> *You are our all in all.*
> *You have become our all in all.*

You have become our provision;
In union with You we have victory.
In You we have died and have risen;
You are our great hope of glory.

197 Andy Park.
Copyright © 1991 Mercy Publishing/
Kingsway's Thankyou Music.

YOU HAVE CALLED US CHOSEN,
A royal priesthood,
A holy nation,
We belong to You.
(Repeat)

> *Take our lives as a sacrifice;*
> *Shine in us Your holy light.*
> *Purify our heart's desire;*
> *Be to us a consuming fire.*

You have shown us mercy,
You have redeemed us;
Our hearts cry "Father,
We belong to You."
(Repeat)

198 Brian Thiessen.
Copyright © 1991 Mercy Publishing/
Kingsway's Thankyou Music.

YOU HAVE SHOWN ME favour unending;
You have given Your life for me.
And my heart knows of Your goodness,
Your blood has covered me.

> *I will arise and give thanks to You, Lord,*
>   *my God,*
> *And Your name I will bless with my*
>   *whole heart.*
> *You have shown mercy, You have*
>   *shown mercy to me.*
> *I give thanks to You, Lord.*

You have poured out Your healing upon us;
You have set the captives free.
And we know it's not what we've done,
But by Your hand alone.

> *We will arise and give thanks to You,*
>   *Lord, our God,*
> *And Your name we will bless with all our*
>   *hearts.*
> *You have shown mercy, You have*
>   *shown mercy to us.*
> *We give thanks to You, Lord.*

You, O Lord, are the healer of my soul.
You, O Lord, are the gracious Redeemer,
You come to restore us again.
Yes, You come to restore us again, and
again.

199

Kevin Prosch & Tom Davis.
Copyright © 1991 Mercy Publishing/
Kingsway's Thankyou Music.

YOU HAVE TAKEN THE PRECIOUS
From the worthless and given us
Beauty for ashes, love for hate.
You have chosen the weak things
Of the world to shame that which is strong,
And the foolish things to shame the wise.

You are help to the helpless,
Strength to the stranger,
And a father to the child that's left alone.
And the thirsty You've invited
To come to the waters,
And those who have no money, come and
    buy.

So come, so come.
So come, so come.

Behold the days are coming,
For the Lord has promised,
That the ploughman will overtake the
    reaper.
And our hearts will be the threshing floor,
And the move of God we've cried out for
Will come, it will surely come.

For You will shake the heavens,
And fill Your house with glory,
And turn the shame of the outcast into
    praise.
And all creation groans and waits
For the Spirit and the bride to say
The word that Your heart has longed to
    hear.

200

Peggy Caswell.
Copyright © 1990 Sound Truth Publishing/
Kingsway's Thankyou Music.

YOUR LOVE O LORD, it reaches to the
    heavens;
Your faithfulness, it reaches to the skies.
Your righteousness is like the mighty
    mountains;
How priceless is Your faithful love.

I will exalt You, O Lord.
I will exalt You, O Lord.
Praise Your holy name,
That my heart may sing to You;
I will exalt You, O Lord.

Your name, O Lord, it is a mighty tower;
Your glory, it covers all the earth.
In Your hands alone are strength and
    power,
All praise be to Your glorious name.

Index of titles and first lines

(Titles where different from first lines, are shown in *italics*)

Song no.

All consuming fire 1
All I once held dear 2
All that I am 3
All that we need 196
All the ends of the earth . . . 4
All the glory 115
And He shall reign 5
Anointing, fall on me 6
Arms of love 71
Army of God 172
As we behold You 7
At the cross 63
At the foot of the cross . . . 8
Awaken the dawn 148
Awaken the nations 4
Awesome God 39

Be free 9
Behold the Lord 10
Be known to us in breaking bread . 11
Because of the Lord's great love. . 186
Blessèd be the name of the Lord . 12
Blessèd Jesus 13
Bless the Lord, my soul . . . 14
Break our hearts 152
Breathe on me 15
Busy little house 131
But if we walk in the light . . . 16

Called to a battle 17
Carry the fire 69
Children of the great King . . . 179
Clap your hands all you nations . . 18
Closer to You 19
Come, Holy Spirit 20
Come into the heavenlies . . . 21
Come, let us return 22
Come, let us worship Jesus . . . 23
Come, Lord Jesus 42

Song no.

Come, Lord Jesus, come 70
Come, my soul, and praise the Lord . 24
Come to the light 66
Cry of my heart 75

Deep calls to deep 25
Don't be lazy 26
Eternity 79
Every time I think of You 27

Faithful God 28
Father I come to You 29
Father, I love You 73
Father me 123
Fill the earth 195
5000+ hungry folk 30
Focus my eyes 31
For the sake of the multitudes . . 32
Friend of sinners 88
From Your throne, O Lord . . . 33

Give your thanks to the risen Son . 34
Glorify 35
Go in Your name 104
God is so good 36
God of heaven 37
God, our God blesses us . . . 38
God You are an awesome God . . 39
Goliath 40
Go to all nations 41
Great is the darkness 42

Hang on 43
Have you got an appetite? . . . 44
Heart of a lover 37
He has been given 45
He has risen 46
He is lovely 47
He is the Lord 48

Song no.

He made the earth 49
He reigns 50
He saves *112*
Holiness is Your life in me 51
Holy and awesome *80*
Holy Ghost 52
Holy Ground *160*
Holy, holy, holy is the Lord . . . 53
Holy is Your name 54
Holy One 55
Holy Spirit 56
Holy Spirit move within me . . . 57
Holy wind of God *141*
How sweet the name of
  Jesus sounds 58
How wonderful 59

I believe there is a God in heaven . 60
I bow down 61
I delight in You, Lord 62
I give thanks *198*
I know a place 63
I love You Lord, my strength . . . 64
I'm a believer *126*
I'm justified *111*
I'm looking up to Jesus 65
I'm standing here to testify . . . 66
In every circumstance 67
In His eyes *53*
In mystery reigning 68
In these days of darkness 69
Into the darkness 70
I sing a simple song of love . . . 71
I sing praises to Your name . . . 72
I stand amazed 73
It is good to give thanks to the Lord . 74
It is the cry of my heart 75
I've got the life of God in me . . . 76
I waited patiently 77
I was made to praise You 78
I will be Yours 79
I will exalt You, O Lord . . . *200*
I will extol the Lord 80
I will give thanks to the Lord . . . 81
I will praise You 82
I will praise You with the harp . . 83
I will wait 84
I will wave my hands 85
I worship You, O Lord 86

Jesus 87
Jesus (*Friend of sinners*) 88

Song no.

Jesus, forgive me 89
Jesus, I am thirsty 90
Jesus is our God *91*
Jesus is the name we honour . . . 91
Jesus, restore to us 92
Jubilee song *176*

King of the nations *23*
Knowing You *2*

La Alleluia *129*
Let every tribe and every tongue . . 93
Let the Bride say come *166*
Let's join together 94
Let the righteous sing 95
Let us draw near 96
Let Your kingdom come . . . *105*
Let Your word 97
Lift Him high *98*
Lift Him up 98
Living sacrifice *109*
Lord of every man *128*
Lord over all *86*
Lord, I have heard of Your fame . . 99
Lord, I lift Your name on high . . 100
Lord Jesus, You are faithful . . 101
Lord, look upon my need 102
Lord of all creation 103
Lord, we come in adoration . . . 104
Lord, You are calling 105
Lord, You are worthy 106
Lord, You have my heart 107

Many will see *77*
May God be gracious to us . . . 108
May our worship 109
May the peoples praise You . . *108*
Mighty God 110
More of You *90*
Most Holy Judge 111
Mourning into dancing *184*
Mukti Dilaye 112
My desire *167*
My God is so big 113
My heart 114
My heart is full 115
My hope is built 116
My lips shall praise You 117

Never gonna stop *27*
Never let my heart grow cold . . . 118
New covenant people 119

Song no.

No eye has seen.	120
No other name	121
Nothing shall separate us	122
O Father of the fatherless	123
O God, be my strength.	124
O God, Most High	125
Oh, I believe in Jesus	126
O Holy One of Israel	*83*
O Lamb of God	127
O Lord, arise.	128
O Lord, I want to sing Your praises	129
O Lord, You're great	130
O most high	*81*
Once there was a house	131
On Christ the solid Rock	*116*
Only one thing	132
Only the blood	*51*
O righteous God.	133
O Spirit of God, come down	134
Our Father in heaven	135
Our God	*49*
Over and over again	*194*
Pour out Your Spirit	*146*
Power from on high	136
Praise and glory.	137
Precious child	*147*
Psalm 47	*18*
Psalm 138	*82*
Quiet my mind	138
Raise up a church	*155*
Rejoice, you sons of Israel	139
Remember mercy	*99*
Restorer of my soul.	*117*
Revelation 7:12	*137*
Rise up	140
Ruach.	141
Sacrifice of love	*158*
Salvation belongs to our God.	142
Save us, O God	*173*
Say the word.	143
Seek righteousness.	144
Send me out from here.	145
Shining forth is Your mercy	146
Shout to the Lord	*170*
Show me, dear Lord	147
Show Your power	*48*
Sing to the Lord.	148

Song no.

Siyahamba	*171*
So come	*199*
Sound the trumpet	149
Speak now, Jesus	150
Take me in.	*151*
Take me past the outer courts.	151
Take our lives	*197*
Teach us, O Lord	152
Tender mercy.	*159*
The crucible for silver	153
The Lord fills me with His strength	154
The Lord has spoken	155
The Lord reigns.	156
The Lord's prayer	*135*
The Lord will rescue me	157
The precious blood of Jesus	158
There is a home.	159
There is holy ground	160
There is none like You.	161
There's no one like You	162
There's nothing I like better	163
The sky is filled	164
This is my belovèd Son	165
This is our heartcry.	*178*
This is the mystery.	166
This land	*185*
Thunder in the skies	*17*
To be in Your presence.	167
Touch my lips.	168
To Your majesty.	169
Unending love	*29*
We are His people	170
We are marching.	171
We are the army of God	172
We confess the sins of our nation.	173
We give thanks	174
We give You praise.	*93*
We have a vision	175
We have called on You, Lord.	176
We hear the cry of the cities	*32*
Welcome, King of kings	177
We're standing here with open hearts	178
We've got a lot of hope	179
We want to see Jesus lifted high.	180
We will tear down every stronghold	181
We will worship the Lamb of glory	182
What kind of love is this?	183
Where there once was only hurt.	184

Song no.

Whose lips will plead 185

Yet this will I call to mind 186
You are good. *189*
You are mighty 187
You are my King. 188
You are righteous 189
You are the great I AM. . . . 190
You are the one and only God . . 191
You are wonderful 192
You are worthy to receive 193

Song no.

You bless my life. 194
You came. 195
You came from heaven to earth . . *100*
You have become for us wisdom. . 196
You have broken the chains . . . *125*
You have called us chosen . . . 197
You have shown me 198
You have taken the precious . . . 199
You're my stronghold *64*
Your love, O Lord 200